DISCOVERED
TREASURES

A Reflection of
ARIZONA COOKING

Text by James E. Cook

LEISURE
TIME
PUBLISHING
INC.
DALLAS,TX

Published by the Arizona Department of Agriculture in conjunction with the Agri-Business Council of Arizona, Phoenix, Arizona, and in association with Leisure Time Publishing, a division of Heritage Worldwide, Incorporated, Dallas, Texas.

Publisher   Rodney L. Dockery
General Manager & Editorial Director   Caleb Pirtle III
Executive Editor   Ken Lively
Managing Editor   Sheri Harris

Regional Publishing Director   P.K. Dailey
Project Editor   Betty Miser
Food Editor   Diane Luther
Editorial Assistant   Susan Lee
Art Director   Lynn Herndon Sullivan
Production Coordinator   Kathy Hazel
Production Manager   Vickie Craig

Photography provided by the Arizona Office of Tourism, the Phoenix & Valley of the Sun Convention & Visitors Bureau, the Salt River Project, the Metropolitan Tucson Convention & Visitors Bureau, and © photos by Thomas Wiewandt, Eddie Goldbaum Rios, C. Cupito and courtesy of Eglin Studios.

Cover Photograph: Red Rock Crossing, Oak Creek. Courtesy of the Arizona Office of Tourism.

First Printing

Manufactured in the United States of America

Printed by:
Heritage Worldwide, Inc.
9029 Directors Row
Dallas, Texas 75247
Telephone: (214) 630-4300

II

CONTENTS

ACKNOWLEDGEMENTS

Our thanks to the following associations who were so kind to contribute their recipes to this book:

Arizona Aquaculture Association
Arizona Beef Council
Arizona Beekeepers Association
Arizona Pistachio Association
Arizona Vegetable Growers
Arizona Wool Producers Association
Colorado River Indian Tribe
United Dairymen of Arizona

We also wish to thank Sunkist®, who markets over 70% of Arizona's citrus, for their recipes, and to the many individuals and businesses who also contributed.

Special thanks to Susan Nunn of the Agri-Business Council, for her hours of help in coordinating this project.

FOREWORD

Arizona—rugged and unyielding in its landscape, rich with unadulterated beauty–the heart of the Great American Southwest.

A land with a distinct heritage.

And flavor.

It is a hearty state laced with the diversity of many cultures, formed by many cultures.

The spirit of Arizona's heritage is reflected in *Discovered Treasures*.

The recipes all have the unique Arizona flavor.

They were prepared for us by those Arizona food manufacturers, agricultural commodity groups and trade associations who are an integral, vibrant part of the Arizona economy.

The recipes mirror the best cooking that Arizona has to offer. They were developed by Arizonans for Arizonans, using Arizona-made food products.

In addition, *Discovered Treasures* provides narrative on scenic, historic and recreational Arizona, ably penned by James E. Cook, one of the state's most noted and widely-read authors.

Discovered Treasures simply gives you more than two hundred new reasons—with more than two hundred recipes—to use Arizona products every time you go to the kitchen to prepare a family meal.

That's good for the state.

And more importantly, that's good for you and your family.

So sit back and savor this book. It's a dash of the Old West, a sip of clear water, a breath of fresh air, a taste of Arizona. Enjoy!

MAGNIFICENT CONTRADICTIONS

"The arable land of the Territory is not extensive when compared with its whole area; but the fertile and well watered valleys of the Gila, the Salado, and the Verde have once, and will again, support a large population. The climate of northern and central Arizona is unsurpassed . . . For grazing it is unequalled."

—John N. Goodwin, first governor of Arizona Territory,
addressing the legislature in September, 1864.

D ry air helps preserve things, including prehistoric ruins. Several of Arizona's ancient towns are national monuments, and even the casual tourist soon begins to piece together facts of The Great Disappearance.

Relatively sophisticated people lived here: the Sinagua at Wupatki and other sites in northern Arizona's plateau country, and in the Verde Valley; their neighbors the Anasazi at Canyon de Chelly and Navajo National Monuments.

Along the shallow rivers of central and southern Arizona, the Hohokam left networks of irrigation canals. Their fields must have spread an inviting shade of green into the desert, beyond the narrow band of trees which normally grew along the Salado (the Salt) and the Gila. The Hohokam are remembered at Casa Grande Ruins National Monument and a Phoenix city park called Pueblo Grande.

These ancients all "vanished" in the years between 1200 A.D. and the mid-1400s. That is to say, evidence of their cultures ends there, leaving intriguing ruins and a suspicion that their descendants are today's Native Americans.

Archaeologists and anthropologists suspect that some disaster befell the ancients' food supply: a long drought, probably, maybe combined with some soil erosion. Many a professor would trade his tenure for the right to be first to prove what happened.

So far as we know, famine hasn't been a problem here since the 1400s. Arizonans learned to feed themselves and a good many others, a testament to the determination and imagination of those who came in waves to settle this paradoxical land.

Nature endowed Arizona with great variety of terrain, a sampler of the continent's geographic wonders. It has been suggested the state was built with odd components that God had left over after six arduous days. The mismatched parts are bound together by arbitrary boundaries and by a sense of place that attaches to Arizona's legends.

Although Arizona's vast deserts are not so monotonous as newcomers expect, some are bleak enough. Love of the desert, or at least fascination with its surprisingly complex life, is an acquired taste.

Broad plateaus, and plateaus upon plateaus, provide a host for some of the world's prettiest canyons, wrinkles in the face of time. The mother of them all, of course, is Grand Canyon.

Arizona is seldom depicted as a mountain state, yet there is hardly a place out of sight of mountains. The tallest reaches 12,643 feet. Some of Arizona's smaller mountains might be national parks if they were suddenly placed among the worn-down nubbins of New England.

The state's central highlands, a rumpled region running southeast to northwest, supports the largest stand of ponderosa pine in the world, not to mention fir and spruce and Gambel oak.

There is a spread of more than two miles' elevation between Arizona's lowest point, south of Yuma, and the highest peak, north of Flagstaff. Arizona has six climatic "life zones," although the zone labeled "arctic-alpine" on the schematic charts is a bit scant.

Climate? Now here's a sensitive point.

There's no denying that it gets hotter than the hinges of your barbecue cooker on Arizona deserts.

An old Pima Indian legend says if someone picks up a Gila monster in summer, the temperature will become unbearably hot. On June 26, 1990, Arizonans figured a Pima had picked up a Gila monster for sure. The temperature reached a record 122 degrees in Phoenix that afternoon, and made the evening news on national TV.

Towns along the Colorado River—Lake Havasu City and Bullhead City, mainly—engage in a masochistic competition to beat out Death Valley, California, as the hottest place in the nation.

"But Arizona has a *dry* heat," people say, and that is true as far as it goes. Even Bostonians have heard that a lack of humidity makes Arizona one of the few places where the apparent temperature is lower than the actual temperature.

Dry heat means dry everything else, of course, a problem Arizona farmers and ranchers have faced for centuries. Writing in the exaggerated style of the 1870s, Captain John G. Bourke described "the supposed junction of the sandbed of the Aravaypa with the sandbed of the San Pedro, which complacently figured on the topographical charts of the time as creek and river respectively, but generally were as dry as a lime-burners hat, excepting during the 'rainy season.'"

Yet in the winter of 1972 and 1973 it snowed 400 inches at Hawley Lake in the mountains of eastern Arizona, sometimes the coldest reporting weather station in the country. Not far away, there was an 11.40-inch rain during one 24-hour period in 1970.

That's the story of Arizona's climate: too much, or too little. Drought or flood. Blazing heat or brittle cold.

And one hundred years ago, a bad reputation. General William Tecumseh Sherman is said to have remarked, "We fought one war with Mexico to win Arizona, and we ought to fight another war to get her to take it back."

Mary Sloan Wilbur, daughter of Arizona's last territorial governor, told me in a 1990 interview that pioneers were reputed to have fled to Arizona only because of "a break in health, a break in wealth, or a break in reputation." An exaggeration—you have to have a sense of humor to conquer a wilderness—but it was based in truth. Her father, Richard E. Sloan, sought the dry air for relief from asthma.

Whatever their credentials, the diverse pioneers turned the extremes of climate and geology to their benefit. Benign desert winters nurture a tourist trade that surpasses the summertime visits to the cool mountains and plateaus of the north. Arizona is one of the world's most popular travel desinations.

What Nature did not provide here was an abundance of land where dry farming could be practiced, or where irrigation was easy.

But when river dams and irrigation canals made farming possible, the native warmth provided farmers a bonus: an extra growing season or two. They can provide broccoli to New York (and Plymouth, Massachussets) in time for Thanksgiving. Yuma's winter seed farmers see to it that farmers in the upper Midwest have cabbage seed on hand as soon as the ground thaws.

We don't often read of the great vegetables of history, but the diaries of Arizona's early European explorers show a preoccupation with feeding themselves, second only to their preoccupation with finding gold. Plainly, they had to work at getting a square meal.

First there were Spaniards. A Jesuit named Fray Marcos de Niza penetrated the Southwest in 1539. He returned to Mexico with fanciful tales of golden cities to the north.

That so intrigued the viceroy of New Spain that he sent Captain Francisco Vasquez de Coronado north with an expedition in 1540. Coronado found only frightened, and therefore hostile, Zunis and Hopis.

One of Coronado's literate soldiers, who kept a diary, reported on the Zuni village of Hawikuh: "There we found something we prized more than gold or silver; namely, plentiful maize and beans, turkeys larger than those in New Spain, and salt better and whiter than any I had ever seen."

Sporadically over the next two centuries, Spanish expeditions probed the frontier. They looked mostly for gold, and for new routes to the Pacific. Father Eusebio Francisco Kino is generally credited with introducing Christianity to the region in 1691; he also introduced the Piman peoples of southern Arizona to cattle ranching in 1697. (Actually, missionaries from New Mexico had begun penetrating the Hopi villages in 1628, but the Hopis steadfastly rejected Christianity.)

Kino and other missionaries instilled their version of civilization in the natives for a time. In the 1700s, however, the Pimas rebelled twice, ejecting Spanish missionaries. That led Spain to establish two outposts in what would one day be Arizona: *presidios* (garrisons) at Tubac in 1752 and at Tucson in 1775, the year the American Revolution began in New England.

They were tiny outposts, at the frayed end of supply lines. Settlers lived more like Native Americans than their countrymen farther south. They subsisted on beef, mutton and what grain and vegetables they could grow on small farms watered from the Santa Cruz River.

In 1776, Captain Juan Bautista de Anza passed through Tubac and Tucson with an expedition that would found the city of San Francisco, California. Perhaps because of that odd historical fact, writers tend to make too much or too little of the Hispanic period in Arizona history. At its peak, there were perhaps 1,000 Hispanic settlers in the region. That was about 1820, when Spain was yielding to Mexico in the revolution that began in 1810. Mexico was even less prepared to provision its distant outposts. Apache raids often forced ranchers and farmers along the Santa Cruz and San Pedro rivers to abandoned their enterprises and retreat southward.

Make no mistake: Hispanic influence on Arizona is profound. But

much of it occurred after the land belonged to the United States, when Mexicans returned or migrated to Arizona.

Beginning in 1825, Mountain Men from the U.S. penetrated the area, trapping for furs. Most traveled the Gila River, which heads up in New Mexico and flows west across Arizona to enter the Colorado River at Yuma.

James Ohio Pattie traveled the Gila in 1825 and 1826, and wrote the first English description of the area. After Indians stole the first expedition's furs and horses, Pattie wrote of seven trappers surviving on the meat of one raven.

On the second expedition, he described the Pima Villages, southeast of modern Phoenix, which would become a critical supply point for explorers during the next forty years. Of the Pimas, Pattie wrote, "They are to a considerable degree cultivators, raising wheat, corn and cotton, which they manufacture into cloths."

The United States acquired Arizona in two stages: the land north of the Gila by the Treaty of Guadalupe Hidalgo in 1848, concluding the Mexican War, and the southern portion through the Gadsden Purchase of 1854.

During the Mexican war, the Pima Villages provisioned two armies of Americans en route to California: Colonel Stephen Watts Kearny's Army of the West, and Captain Philip St. George Cooke's Mormon Battalion. Pimas sold them cornmeal, flour, pumpkins, melons, beans.

Still, the dining was not sumptuous. On Christmas Day, 1846, a private in the Mormon Batallion wrote in his diary: "Traveled twenty miles and camped without water. Traveled through a sandy desert. Ate our Christmas supper by the roadside. Had cold beans, pancakes, and pumpkin sauce."

Arizona was at first a part of New Mexico Territory, created in 1850 (Arizona became a separate territory in 1863). The Gadsden Purchase added the land below the Gila in 1854.

American adventurers flocked to the region between 1854 and the

White Mountains near Mogollon Rim

start of the Civil War, looking for gold and silver. Tubac was a center of *Yanqui* mining activity. Tucson began to blossom as a commercial center. The Butterfield Stage ran through the area briefly, but its route was moved northward at the beginning of the Civil War. Federal troops were withdrawn eastward.

Captain Sherod Hunter, a farmer at Mesilla, New Mexico, became a Confederate captain in charge of securing the newly-proclaimed Confederate State of Arizona. He "captured" Tucson with a troop of about sixty-five volunteers. Then his soldiers captured a flour mill at the Pima Villages, hoping to deprive approaching Union soldiers.

But the volunteer California Column, nearly 2,000 strong, drove Hunter and his troops back to New Mexico. Three of Colonel James H. Carleton's advancing troops were killed when they stumbled into Hunter's rear guard at Picacho Pass April 16, 1862, the only "battle" of the Civil War in Arizona.

Conventional wisdom says that when the Lincoln administration appointed a party of political hangers-on to establish territorial government in 1863, it directed them to find a new capital because Tucson was a hotbed of southern sympathy. But letters and diaries from members of the party show they were guided as much by the lure of gold as by any desire to set up a new government.

Thus Arizona's first capital city, Prescott, was established on Granite Creek in the Bradshaw Mountains, where gold had recently been discovered. Territorial Supreme Court Justice Joseph P. Allyn wrote in the spring of 1864: "No one knows what the seasons are, or how much rain we have. Still a good many acres are spaded up and a little of everything is being planted. If anything grows it will be remunerative, for anything in the shape of a vegetable will bring any price, there being none here."

Provisions had to be freighted in from Santa Fe, or shipped up the Colorado River from the Gulf of California, then freighted inland. Flour and coffee cost one dollar a pound—when they could be purchased. Sometimes weeks passed between freight wagons.

Historian Pauline Henson quotes prospector Thomas D. Sanders, who recalled surviving for three weeks on venison: "We decided to make the best of it and by doling out the little salt we had left, we cooked our venison in every conceivable manner. We had it fried, boiled, stewed, baked and barbecued. Three weeks of this grew frightfully tiresome."

Someone had to provision the growing number of miners and soldiers in the raw territory, and that's how Phoenix came to be. In the middle 1860s, former soldier John Smith was growing wild hay along the Salt River and selling it to the army at nearby Fort McDowell.

Jack Swilling was farming at the new mining boomtown of Wickenburg, fifty miles northwest, and looking for new opportunities. Swilling had been a member of Sherod Hunter's Confederate volunteers, and later a member of the Walker Party which discovered gold in the Prescott area.

He organized an irrigation company to take water from the Salt and deliver it to new farmlands. In places, Swilling's workers used old canals abandoned by the Hohokam in the 1400s. A new townsite was established in 1870 and Phoenix began to roll toward it's 1990s destiny: eighth largest city in the nation.

Transcontinental railroads spanned Arizona in the 1870s and 1880s: Southern Pacific in the south, Atlantic & Pacific (Santa Fe) in the north. Both missed Phoenix, but by 1895 branch lines had been built into the city. Its aggressive irrigators and promoters succeeded in making Phoenix the capital in 1889. One inducement to rural legislators was a selection of new hotels with dining rooms provisioned from local farms, and by rail from elsewhere.

Linked by rail to the rest of the world, Phoenix became trade center for a diverse economy, and an even more diverse population. Mines switched from gold and silver to copper, and the big copper camps like Bisbee and Clifton and Jerome drew citizens from the Old World: eastern Europe, Ireland, Cornwall, Wales.

Cattle ranching grew in every corner of the state. Mormon farmers and ranchers were dispatched south from Utah to spread their church's influence. Southerners, disenchanted with Reconstruction, headed west. English and Scotch remittance men, second or third in line to inherit estates in their homelands, opted to ranch in Arizona.

Arizona became the forty-eighth state on February 14, 1912. Only a few months before, the completion of Theodore Roosevelt Dam northeast of Phoenix had guaranteed a stable supply of water. The boosters of Phoenix recruited thousands of farm families from the Midwest.

Having addressed the problems of drought and flood, Arizonans set out to do something about the weather. Desert heat was still intolerable, and commerce slowed to a crawl in summer. The evaporative cooler evolved slowly, but its use suddenly mushroomed in the late 1930s. In the spring of 1936 a Phoenix newspaper published a special section to celebrate this new industry.

Even before the United States was drawn into World War II, the military and Arizona's boosters saw that sunny weather and wide open spaces provided an ideal training ground for fighting men. Hundreds of thousands of airmen and ground soldiers trained for combat at dozens of bases in Arizona. Farmers, bereft of much of their labor supply, found a new source: they could rent German and Italian prisoners of war from nearby prison camps.

Many World War II trainees returned after the war. The nation's westward tilt was speeded by mechanical cooling and a new mobility. Others heard the word and followed, in an unprecedented population boom that only slows periodically, then accelerates again. Two out of three Arizonans were born elsewhere.

Now here's another of those paradoxes which make Arizona difficult to describe: It is one of the most urbanized states. More than half its population lives in the several cities of Maricopa County, where Phoenix is located; another twenty percent lives in the Tucson area.

Yet the people think of themselves as Arizonans, rather than residents of a particular city. At every opportunity they make a break for the state's open spaces—the mountains, the canyons, the deserts.

APPETIZERS & SNACKS

Canyon de Chelly

Frijoles Y Queso Con Guacamole

1 (16 oz) can refried beans
2 ripe avocados, pureed
1 cup sour cream
1 cup grated UDA Seal of Arizona Mild Cheddar Cheese
1 (2.25 oz) can ripe sliced olives
1 cup chopped cilantro
1 jar Big Juan's Hot or Mild Fresh Salsa
Arizona Brand® Tortilla Chips

- Spread beans over large platter, ¼" thick; pour avocado on top.
- Spread sour cream over avocado, being careful not to blend.
- Sprinkle thin layer cheese over sour cream, then olives. Sprinkle cilantro on top.
- Spread salsa ¼" thick.
- Serve with tortilla chips.
- Serves 6-8.

Hot Cowboy Salami Snacks

1 (8 oz) pkg crescent rolls
1 (8 oz) Cowboy Quiltie Salami, thinly sliced
Cactus Desert Mustard
grated Cowboy Cheese

Chili Dip:
1 cup sour cream
2 tbsp mayonnaise
½ tbsp Authentic Cowboy Chili Seasoning

- Preheat oven to 375 degrees.
- Unroll dough into 4 rectangles. Firmly press perforations to seal.
- Place salami slices on rectangles and spread with mustard.
- Starting at shortest side, roll; press edges to seal. Cut each roll into 5 slices.
- Place cut side down on ungreased cookie sheet.
- Bake 15-20 minutes until golden brown. Immediately remove from cookie sheet.
- Sprinkle lightly with grated cheese.
- Serve warm.
- To make chili dip, mix together well sour cream, mayonnaise and chili seasoning.
- Chill 1 hour before serving with salami snacks.
- Makes 20.

Eggplant Rolls Stuffed with Goat Cheese

2 medium eggplants
1 tsp salt
1½ cups olive oil
4 oz goat cheese
4 oz UDA Seal of Arizona Cream Cheese
⅓ cup red wine vinegar
2 cloves Rhee's Garlic, minced
⅓ cup chopped Rhee's Italian Parsley
⅓ cup fresh chopped basil
salt and freshly ground pepper

- Slice unpeeled eggplant lengthwise into ⅜" thick slices; sprinkle with salt, drain on paper towels at least 30 minutes. Pat slices dry.
- Heat 2 tbsp olive oil in large sauté pan.
- Add ¼ of eggplant slices; sauté until golden brown, 2-3 minutes per side.
- Remove; drain on paper towels.
- Sauté remaining eggplant slices, adding 2 tbsp olive oil with each batch. Drain slices on paper towels.
- Mix goat cheese and cream cheese together until smooth.
- Spread each slice of eggplant with 2 tbsp of cheese mixture; roll into a cylinder.
- Place rolls, seam side down, in shallow glass dish.
- In a small bowl, whisk remaining olive oil, vinegar, garlic, parsley and basil.
- Season with salt and pepper to taste; pour over the eggplant rolls to marinate.
- Chill at least 24 hours, or up to 4 days; serve at room temperature.
- Makes 2 doz.

Pancho Villa Dip

1 (16 oz) can refried beans
½ cup Desert Rose Medium Red Salsa
1 cup grated UDA Seal of Arizona Monterey Jack or Colby Cheese

- Mix ingredients together.
- Serve hot or cold.
- Makes 3 cups.

Pickle Chips

vegetable oil for frying
1 Hickman's Egg
2 tbsp sweet pickle liquid
½ cup dry bread crumbs
1 tsp onion salt
1 cup Arnold's Sweet Pickle Chips, well drained
3 tbsp all-purpose flour

- Heat 1″ oil in heavy skillet to 375 degrees.
- Combine egg and pickle liquid.
- Combine bread crumbs and onion salt.
- Coat each pickle slice with flour. Dip in egg mixture, then in bread crumbs.
- Fry in small batches, 1½ minutes, or until browned, turning once.
- Remove with slotted spoon; drain on paper towels. Serve immediately.
- Makes 2½ doz.

Southwestern Dip

1 (8 oz) pkg cream cheese, softened
3 green onions, with tops
1 (8 oz) can stewed tomatoes, well drained
1½ tsp Mad Coyote Salsa Mix
bagels or assorted crackers

- Blend cream cheese until smooth.
- Chop green onions; add to cream cheese along with remaining ingredients.
- Refrigerate at least 6 hours for best flavor.
- Serve on bagels or crackers.
- Makes 2 cups.

Chi-Wow-Wow! Bean Dip

2 (16 oz) cans Rosarita® Refried Beans
3 cups shredded Cheddar cheese
2 cups shredded Monterey Jack cheese
1 (16 oz) jar Rosarita® Mild Chunky Picante Sauce
1 (4.5 oz) can chopped ripe black olives
1 (4 oz) can diced green chilies
½ cup sliced green onion
½ tsp garlic powder
½ tsp salt
¼ cup chopped cilantro
Territorial Gourmet Blue Corn Tortilla Chips

- In large saucepan, combine all ingredients except tortilla chips.
- Heat, stirring frequently, until cheese is melted and beans are bubbling.
- Serve with tortilla chips for dipping.
- Makes 8 cups.

Red Chile Pepper Dip

½ cup Cheri's Red Chile Pepper Jelly
1 (8 oz) pkg cream cheese
¼ tsp red chili flakes (optional)
Desert Rose Tortilla Chips

- Blend jelly with room temperature cream cheese until well blended.
- For more heat, add red chili flakes and stir.
- Serve with tortilla chips.
- Makes 1½ cups.

Dilly Dip

1 cup mayonnaise
1 cup Shamrock® Sour Cream
1-2 tbsp Mannons Dilly Dip, Fiesta!, Hot Potato, Wow-Garlic, Viva! Jalapeno or Cajun Cookin' Mix

- Mix all ingredients together.
- Makes 2 cups.

Guacamole

3 large ripe avocados
½ cup Mad Coyote Salsa
dash celery salt
1½ tbsp lemon juice
Blue Corn Connection Blue Corn Chips

- In large mixing bowl, peel, pit and coarsely mash avocados.
- Add salsa, celery salt and lemon juice; leave mixture chunky.
- Serve with chips.
- Makes 2 cups.

Eggplant Caviar

1 medium eggplant
2 tbsp olive oil
1 cup Desert Rose Red Salsa
½-1 tsp powdered sugar
salt and pepper
assorted crackers

- Bake eggplant 45 minutes at 350 degrees.
- Cool; remove skin and chop pulp.
- Sauté in olive oil.
- Add salsa and remaining ingredients.
- Simmer 15-20 minutes, uncovered.
- Serve with crackers.
- Makes 3 cups.

Salsa Sandwich Spread

½ cup Miguel's Original Home Style or Southwestern Gourmet Salsa
1 (8 oz) pkg cream cheese, softened

- Mix salsa into cream cheese.
- Delicious as a dip, spread for crackers or in place of mayonnaise on bread to make sandwiches.
- Makes 1½ cups.

Seasoned Popcorn Delight

4 cups popped Kachina White Popcorn

Kachina Popcorn Jalapeno, Sour Cream and Onion, Classic Italian or Chili and Cheese Seasoning

- Shake seasonings on popcorn.
- Toss and eat.
- Serves 2-4.

Fire and Spice Nuts

½ tsp cumin
½ tsp chili powder
½ tsp curry powder
½ tsp garlic salt
¼ tsp garlic powder
¼ tsp cayenne
¼ tsp powdered ginger
¼ tsp cinnamon
2 tbsp olive oil
2 cups shelled, whole The Pecan Store Pecans
1 tbsp coarse salt (optional)

- Preheat oven 325 degrees.
- Mix all spices except coarse salt.
- Set aside.
- Heat oil in non-stick skillet over low heat.
- Add spice mixture and stir well.
- Simmer 3-4 minutes.
- Add nuts to skillet; mix well.
- Spread nuts on baking sheet.
- Bake 15 minutes, shaking once or twice.
- Remove from oven; toss nuts with any leftover spices in bottom of pan.
- Sprinkle with coarse salt, if desired.
- Cool 2 hours.
- Store in airtight jar.
- Makes 2 cups.

Chutnut Cheese Ball

½ lb bleu cheese
1 (16 oz) pkg cream cheese
½ cup chopped Desert Kettle Apricot Chutney
chopped Arizona Nuts Pecans
assorted crackers or small breads

- Mix all ingredients together.
- Shape into 2 large balls.
- Roll each ball in chopped pecans.
- Balls may be frozen.
- Serve with crackers or small breads.
- Serves 12-16.

Cheese Crisp

1 cup grated Colby cheese
Territorial Gourmet Blue Corn Tortilla Chips
½ cup Arizona Champagne Jalapeno Jelly, Hot or Mild

- Spread cheese over tortillas; top with jalapeno jelly.
- Heat under broiler until cheese melts.
- Serves 4-6.

Southwestern Canapes

1 cup sour cream
1 (8 oz) pkg cream cheese
3-4 tbsp Arizona Southwest Mix
12-16 small Arizona Brand® Flour Tortillas

- Mix all ingredients together except tortillas.
- Spread thinly on tortillas and roll up.
- Roll tortillas in wax paper; freeze.
- Slice when ready to serve.
- Serves 30.

Spiced Pecans

¹/₄ cup butter
¹/₂ tbsp Arizona Gunslinger Smokin' Hot Jalapeno Pepper Sauce
1 tbsp Worcestershire sauce
1 tbsp garlic salt
2 cups large Country Estate Pecan Halves

- Melt butter and add seasonings.
- Coat nuts with mixture; toast at 325 degrees 10 minutes.
- Shake nuts occasionally as they toast.
- Drain on brown paper.
- Serves 2-4.

Toasted Sugar Pecans

3 cups Country Estate Pecans
1 cup sugar
¹/₂ cup water
1 tbsp Shamrock® Butter
salt

- In large, heavy skillet, cook pecans, sugar and water; simmering until all water has been absorbed.
- Place pecans on buttered cookie sheet; bake in preheated 300 degree oven 15 minutes, stir.
- Bake 15 minutes longer. Sprinkle with salt.
- Serves 3-6.

Chinese Honey Buns

¼ lb Beck's Ground Pork
½ cup chopped onion
½ cup chopped mushrooms
2 tbsp soy sauce
2 tbsp packed brown sugar
¼ tsp cornstarch
½ cup chopped Triple A Pistachios
1 (32 oz) pkg frozen white bread dough, thawed
2 tbsp honey
¼ cup finely chopped Triple A Pistachios

- Stir-fry pork and onion until pork is browned; add mushrooms and soy sauce.
- Mix sugar and cornstarch; stir into pork mixture.
- Cook until mushrooms are tender.
- Remove from heat; add pistachios.
- Cut bread dough into 56 pieces; flatten into 2″ rounds.
- Place 1 tsp filling in center of each round, gather edges and seal.
- Place sealed-side down on baking sheet.
- Bake at 350 degrees 10-12 minutes, or until golden brown.
- Brush with honey; sprinkle with finely chopped pistachios.
- Makes 56.

Tomato Herb Biscuit Appetizer

1 (12 oz) pkg Territorial Gourmet Tomato Herb Biscuit Mix
1 (4 oz) jar Territorial Gourmet Olé Pesto Sauce
2 ripe tomatoes, thinly sliced
2 oz imported ham, very thinly sliced
freshly ground black pepper

- Make biscuits according to pkg directions, cutting in 1″ rounds.
- Spread cooled biscuits with pesto sauce.
- Top with slice of tomato and a curl of ham.
- Sprinkle with black pepper.
- Serves 12.

Pistachio-Vegetable Appetizer

4 cups Pavo Green, Red and Yellow
Peppers cut into ¾" wide strips

1 cup shredded Monterey Jack cheese

3 tbsp coarsely chopped The Arizona
Pistachio Company Pistachios

1 (4 oz) can diced green chilies

¼ cup finely chopped onion

- Arrange peppers on broiler-proof pan.
- Sprinkle with cheese, pistachios, chilies and onion.
- Broil or bake at 450 degrees until cheese melts.
- Serves 8.

Shish Kebab Garlic Sausage

4 lbs Beck's Ground Pork

12 cloves Rhee's Garlic

¼ tsp ginger

1½ tsp pepper

3 tsp ground fresh Rhee's Sage

2 tsp salt

2 tsp rosemary or rosemary sticks

¼ tsp cayenne

24 slices Beck's Bacon, halved

- Place pork in large bowl; add spices and mix well. If using rosemary skewers, omit fresh rosemary.
- Cover and refrigerate overnight.
- Shape into 1" balls; wrap with bacon strips.
- Place on skewers or rosemary sticks; grill or oven broil 10 minutes, turning once.
- Makes 48.

Smokin' Hot Buffalo Wings

2½ lbs chicken wings

¼ cup Arizona Gunslinger Smokin' Hot
Jalapeno Pepper Sauce

½ cup melted butter

- Split wings at each joint, discard tips, pat dry.
- Mix sauce and butter; dip wings to coat completely.
- Bake in roasting pan at 425 degrees 30 minutes; turn over and bake an additional 30 minutes.
- Serves 12-15.

Sweet and Sour Pistachio Meatballs

1 lb ground Young's Farm Turkey

½ cup fresh bread crumbs

½ cup chopped The Arizona Pistachio Company Pistachios

¼ cup minced onion

1 Laid in Arizona Egg, beaten

dash salt

chopped, shelled pistachios (optional)

Sweet and Sour Sauce:

¾ cup pineapple juice

2 tbsp brown sugar

2 tbsp cider vinegar

4 tsp cornstarch

1 tbsp soy sauce

- Make sweet and sour sauce by combining all ingredients and cooking over low heat, stirring constantly, until thickened.
- Combine turkey, bread crumbs, pistachios, onion, egg and salt.
- Shape into ¾" to 1" balls. Place on 15" x 10¼" x ¾" pan. Bake at 400 degrees 15 minutes, or until cooked.
- Place sweet and sour sauce in large chafing pan or skillet; heat thoroughly. Stir in meatballs to evenly coat.
- Garnish with pistachios.
- Makes 5 doz.

Roasted Pecans

1 tbsp butter

1 cup Country Estate Pecan Halves

½ tbsp Sallie's Saltmix

- Butter cookie sheet.
- Spread pecans on sheet.
- Bake in preheated 300 degree oven 15 minutes; stirring occasionally until pecans are lightly browned.
- Remove from oven.
- Add salt and stir.
- Pecans crisp as they cool.
- Serves 2.

BREADS

Sunset over the Tucson Mountains

Sour Cream Date Coffee Cake

¼ *cup Shamrock® Butter, softened*

1½ *cups sugar*

3 Laid In Arizona Eggs

1 tsp vanilla

3 cups all-purpose flour

1½ *tsp baking soda*

1 cup Shamrock® Sour Cream

Date Filling:

2¼ *cups chopped Sphinx Medjool Dates*

1 cup water

2 tbsp sugar

Streusel Topping:

½ *cup all-purpose flour*

¼ *cup sugar*

½ *tsp cinnamon*

¼ *cup Shamrock® Butter*

½ *cup chopped walnuts*

- To make filling, mix all ingredients in saucepan.
- Cook over low heat, stirring constantly, until thickened; cool.
- Preheat oven to 375 degrees.
- Grease 2, 9″ round cake pans.
- Cream butter and sugar.
- Beat in eggs until mixture is light and fluffy; add vanilla.
- Combine flour and baking soda; add to creamed mixture alternately with sour cream.
- Divide batter evenly in cake pans. Spread date filling on top of batter.
- For topping, combine flour, sugar and cinnamon. Cut in butter until crumbly.
- Sprinkle streusel topping over date filling; top with walnuts.
- Bake 25-30 minutes.
- Serves 14-16.

Fruit 'N' Oat Bran Muffins

1 pkg The Honey Baker Oat Bran Muffin Mix

3 eggs

1¼ *cups cold water*

½ *cup blueberries, drained*

- Place dry ingredients in large mixing bowl.
- Add contents from small packet, eggs and water to dry ingredients.
- Mix well, divide dough into 12 cup greased muffin pan.
- Bake in 375 degree oven 45 minutes.
- Makes 1 doz.

Coffee Pistachio Date Loaf

2 cups sifted all-purpose flour
4 tsp baking powder
1 tsp salt
⅔ cup sugar
⅓ cup chopped Arizona Nuts Pistachios
¾ cup finely cut, pitted Munson's Dates
¼ cup minced candied ginger
1 cup strong Espressions Coffee
⅛ tsp baking soda
1 egg, well beaten
2 tbsp melted shortening

- Mix flour, baking powder, salt and sugar.
- Stir in pistachios, dates and candied ginger.
- Combine coffee, baking soda, egg and shortening.
- Add, all at once, to dry ingredients.
- Stir only enough to dampen dry ingredients.
- Turn into greased loaf pan, 8″ x 5″ x 2″, or straight-sided loaf pan, 4½″ x 11¼″ x 5¾″.
- Let stand 20 minutes.
- Bake at 375 degrees 45 minutes.
- Serves 8-10.

Cheddar Shortbread

1¼ cups all-purpose flour
½ tsp paprika
½ tsp Santa Cruz Coriander
¼ tsp dry mustard
½ cup butter, softened
2 cups shredded UDA Seal of Arizona Cheddar Cheese, at room temperature
½ cup finely chopped Arizona Nuts

- Preheat oven to 400 degrees.
- Combine flour, paprika, coriander and mustard.
- Cream butter; gradually add cheese, beating until well blended.
- Gradually beat in dry ingredients.
- Place dough on lightly buttered cookie sheet.
- Roll into 12″ x 7″ rectangle. Cut into 1″ x 2″ servings. Sprinkle on nuts.
- Bake 12-15 minutes.
- Recut; remove to wire racks to cool.
- Makes 42 squares.

Spicy Cowboy Corn Bread

1 cup Silver Creek Mill Yellow
Corn Meal

¼ cup all-purpose flour

1 tsp baking powder

1 tsp salt

2 tbsp sugar

2 eggs

¾ cup milk

⅓ cup vegetable oil

1 cup cream style corn

¾ cup grated Cowboy Cheese

1 tbsp Authentic Cowboy
Chili Seasoning

- Combine ingredients in bowl; mix until just combined.

- Bake in greased pan at 425 degrees 25 minutes.

- Serves 6-8.

Bake-In Jelly Muffins

2 cups all-purpose flour

¼ cup sugar

3 tsp baking powder

½ tsp salt

¼ cup vegetable oil

1 Hickman's Egg, slightly beaten

1 cup milk

¼ cup Desert Kettle Pyracantha Jelly

- Sift together flour, sugar, baking powder and salt.

- Mix oil, egg and milk; add to dry ingredients, stir until moistened. Batter will be lumpy.

- Fill greased muffin tins half full.

- Place 1 tsp jelly on each; add batter to fill tins ⅔ full.

- Bake at 400 degrees 20-25 minutes.

- Serves 12.

Williams Waterfall cascades with seasonal runoff from White Horse Lake

Italian Sausage Bread Ring

1 (1 lb) loaf frozen bread dough

1 lb mild or hot Barone Italian Sausage

2 eggs

1½ tsp Italian herb seasoning

1½ cups shredded UDA Seal of Arizona
Mozzarella or Jack Cheese

1 tbsp grated Parmesan cheese

- Let bread defrost in refrigerator overnight, or at room temperature 2-2½ hours.

- Fry sausages in covered pan until well done; cut into small pieces.

- Beat 1 egg; add to sausage with seasoning and cheese.

- On lightly floured board, roll and stretch bread dough into 6″ x 18″ rectangle.

- Spoon sausage mixture evenly over dough to within ½″ of edges.

- Starting with a long side, roll up dough, pinch seam firmly to seal.

- On large baking sheet, shape roll into ring. Pinch end together to seal.

- Slash top of ring, making ½″ cuts, 1½″ apart.

- Beat in remaining egg; brush over bread ring; sprinkle with Parmesan cheese.

- Cover; let rise until doubled, about 35 minutes.

- Bake at 350 degrees 30 minutes, or until golden brown.

- Serve warm.

- Serves 12-15.

Honey Orange Muffins

½ cup sifted all-purpose flour
½ tsp salt
2 tsp baking powder
½ cup Silver Creek Mill Stone Ground Whole Wheat Flour
1 egg, well beaten
¼ cup Jackson Orange Juice
1 tsp grated orange rind
½ cup Mountain Top Honey
3 tbsp melted shortening

- Sift flour, salt and baking powder together.
- Add whole wheat flour; mix thoroughly.
- Combine egg, orange juice, rind, honey and shortening.
- Add to flour, stirring only enough to moisten.
- Bake in well greased muffin pans in 400 degree oven 15-20 minutes, or until browned.
- Serves 4-5.

Orange Pecan Bread

1 egg
1 cup Jackson Orange Juice
1 cup finely cut raisins
1 tbsp grated orange rind
2 tbsp melted shortening
1 tsp vanilla
2 cups sifted all-purpose flour
1 tsp baking powder
½ tsp baking soda
¼ tsp salt
1 cup sugar
1 cup chopped Country Estate Pecans

- Beat egg.
- Stir in orange juice, raisins, orange rind, shortening and vanilla.
- Sift flour, baking powder, baking soda, salt and sugar into liquid mixture; mix well.
- Stir in pecans.
- Pour into well greased 9" x 5" loaf pan.
- Bake in preheated 350 degree oven 1 hour.
- Serves 4-5.

Blue Corn Pancakes

1 cup milk
1 Laid In Arizona Egg
1 tbsp oil (double for waffles)
1 cup Mannons Blue Corn Mix

- Mix milk, egg and oil together.
- Add corn mix.
- Do not over mix!
- Cook on skillet or grill.
- Makes approximately 24, 3″ pancakes.

Indian Fry Bread
—Recipe of United Presbyterian Women
Submitted by Colorado River Indian Tribe

3 lbs all-purpose flour
2 tsp salt
4 tbsp baking powder
1 cup shortening
tepid water
shortening to fry

- Knead all ingredients until smooth.
- Add tepid water slowly while continuing kneading dough.
- Dough should be smooth and just firm enough to form into balls about 2½″ in diameter.
- Let balls rise 30 minutes; roll each out on floured board until 6″ in diameter.
- Melt enough shortening to measure 2″-3″ in fry pan.
- Drop gently into hot shortening; turn over when brown on underside.
- Remove from grease when brown and done in center.
- Makes about 36.

NATIVE AMERICANS

"The Pima and Maricopa tribes of Indians, whose joint reservations lie to the south and east of Phoenix, are fine specimens of the American Indian . . . By means of several crooked sticks shaped into the semblance of a plow, attached by ropes to the horns of a cow, they annually seed many thousand acres to Sonora wheat, and irrigate through ditches constructed many years ago with much labor and ingenuity."
                    —*The Arizona Republican*, May 30, 1890.

The story in the daily newspaper used many more paragraphs to describe the Pimas and Maricopas. As condescending as the story seems now, it was a sensitive article for the times.

It had been less than four years since Geronimo surrendered. Many non-Indians still believed that the only good Indian was a dead Indian. That sentiment was usually reserved for the Apaches of eastern Arizona or the Yavapais farther west. White men frequently didn't know the difference between Apaches and Yavapais, but both had bitterly fought the European intrusion into Arizona.

The Pimas and the Maricopas had been generally friendly to

Europeans for almost 300 years. They called the latest newcomers "Medigans," their approximation of the pronunciation of "Americans."

Pimas threshed their wheat by hand and stowed it in granaries. When they needed money they sacked it up, loaded it on a horse and delivered it to a flour mill in Phoenix or Tempe. The residents of the new towns had only one problem with the Piman peoples: the traditional nakedness of the men, who wore only a G-string in summer. Cast-off overalls were placed on trees and fence posts at the perimeter of Phoenix for use by the visitors.

There are almost 200,000 native Americans of more than a dozen tribes on Arizona's twenty-one reservations. The reservations range from seventy-six acres to the size of West Virginia. One native group, the 204-member San Juan Paiutes of northern Arizona, won federal recognition in 1990 as the nation's 509th Indian tribe.

For one hundred years or so, whites were preoccupied with what they thought about the Indians. Only lately have most of the rest of us thought to ask what the natives think of us. To view them as conquered people, in the fashion of 1970s movements, is hardly more useful than the 1870s view.

What is useful, and intriguing, is to look at the ways Native Americans are asserting their own cultures, and what they contribute to the amalgam of Arizona culture.

Historian John S. Gray points out that even the hostile tribes were not so much opponents of the white man's way of life as they were proponents of their own way of life. The "Indians wars" were more than a mere turf dispute. White newcomers seemed so convinced of the effectiveness of their ways of doing things that they could not recognize the validity of Indian cultures. We still call Indian beliefs "myths" or "legends."

Native Americans believed in living in harmony with Mother Earth, harvesting only what they needed to survive. They needed little, and in the fragile environment of the Southwest, Nature had little to give. The philosophy worked fine for natives, whose numbers were kept low by a number of factors, including disease and famine.

But the white man's economic engine demanded constant growth and new fuel to survive. The native did not believe that anyone owned the earth, but a white entrepreneur had to lay claim to the earth to protect his interests.

Natives lived communally in families and clans and bands. Leaders ruled by consensus, and a leader who placed himself above his followers was doomed to be ignored. Some modern Indian politicians, whose tribes have been arbitrarily organized on the lines of white hierarchies, have to deal with conflicting ideas of leadership.

And so the white man came, with arbitrary boundaries and wasteful ways, and rarely any regard to what Indians believed in.

Indians take care of family first, and ambitions second. Thus the reservations of Arizona are havens from the white man's fierce competition. Outsiders are usually welcome there, if they walk softly and employ uncommon courtesy.

When I was younger, and thought I knew a lot about Indians, I frequently visited the Navajo Reservation, which covers Arizona's northeast corner and extends into Utah and New Mexico. It is the largest in the country, with an estimated population of 200,000.

The Navajos and Apaches, Athapascan people originally from Siberia, came south into this region in the 1500s, about the time the Spaniards arrived. While the Navajo Nation is complex and modern in some respects, it also is a society of deeply traditional people and deeply traditional lack of money.

When I was attending an anti-poverty conference at St. Michaels one day, a Navajo leader said, "I'll buy your lunch." He provided a cup of coffee and a round of fry bread. At least I had the sensitivity to not tell him I had my heart set on a cheeseburger at a nearby cafe.

Years later, I realized how typical that meal was. Mutton stew is the preferred dish. When the Army built a Navajo village to help man Navajo Ordnance Depot near Flagstaff during World War II, opportunists from the reservation lined up outside the fence with freshly slaughtered mutton for sale.

But Navajos grow sheep for wool, and it's not always economically feasible to eat the stock in trade. So many Navajos subsisted on fry bread and coffee. So, in fact, did many a white prospector during hard times; fry bread is close kin to the European scone and the Mexican sopapilla.

Navajos also invented the Navajo Taco, a round of fry bread topped with red or green chili con carne and the traditional garnishes of Mexican fiesta foods: lettuce, cheese, onions.

The Navajo Nation has parks and museums and visitor centers at Window Rock and elsewhere, to acquaint visitors with their culture. What is just as interesting is a long drive across the reservation, just to see the vastness. The stark rock formations are usually red or yellow, streaked with "varnish" of rain-washed minerals. But sometimes the nearest mesa is blue with the haze of distance, and the row of mesas beyond that a subtle lavendar, barely visible. Here and there you can still see the traditional dwelling, the six- to eight-sided hogan of logs or stone.

My wife and I later acquired the fry bread habit while attending a Pima tribal fair at Sacaton. While older Pimas did a social dance called "chicken scratch," oblivious to visiting Anglos, we stopped at booths and sampled fry bread offered with various toppings: chili, refried beans, honey and powdered sugar.

Pimas and their neighbors to the south, the Tohono O'odham (Papagoes), are probably descended from the Hohokam who lived here centuries ago. A few years back the Papagoes grew weary of the Spanish name applied to them and asserted their own name for themselves: Tohono O'odam, "desert people."

One oft-repeated Arizona scene, celebrated in photographs and paintings, is of Tohono O'odham with long poles harvesting fruit from the tops of tall saguaros. A traditional coming-of-age ritual for young Papago men required them to run one hundred miles or so to the Gulf of California and return with a supply of salt for cooking.

The paloverde is Arizona's official state tree, and the saguaro bloom is the state flower. But the gnarled mesquite ought to fit in there somewhere. It grows throughout Arizona's lower regions, up to about

5,000 feet elevation. Its hard wood has been useful for centuries; it fired the steamboats on the Colorado River, and some crude, early smelters.

In recent times, mesquite charcoal has been introduced to classy New York restaurants for the distinctive flavor it lends to beef and seafoods. One informant for this text said mesquite is also hot stuff in the restaurants of her native Vancouver, B.C. (The author uses a locally-bottled, mesquite-flavored barbecue sauce for his locally-famous Role Reversal Ribs.)

But mesquite once had a more immediate use in the kitchen. Through the summer and fall, the trees grow heavy with long, yellow seed pods. Natives ground them into a flour essential to their survival. European settlers fed them to their livestock, which irritated the Indians.

Years ago we stopped for soda pop at a trading post on the Hopi reservation, which is entirely surrounded by the Navajo domain. Many of the Hopi villages were built on Mesas for protection against Spaniards, Navajos and Paiutes.

The Hopi trader suggested we would be welcome at a dance soon to begin in a village atop Second Mesa. Respectfully, we sidled into the plaza of the village. The dance was gorgeous and moving. It was here that we were offered our first taste of Hopi piki, a thin bread made with blue corn. Thin batter is cooked on a hot rock or a griddle, and the paper-thin bread is rolled into an ash-blue scroll. Corn is a symbol of life to Hopis, who used their colored varieties in their religious observances. But when our hosts ran out of piki, they passed around bakery white bread as part of the observance.

While Hopis are congenial and not at all threatening, they don't always relish visitors. They have closed some of their religious dances to visitors in recent years. They steadfastly shrugged off Catholicism, whose missionaries began visiting the villages in 1628; in 1700 the Hopis destroyed one village whose occupants had gone over to Christianity. Today, Hopi clans and villages retain their autonomy, despite a tribal-type government.

Visitors are welcome at a cultural center, museum and gift shops along the highways that link the mesas. There you can buy the silverwork called Hopi Overlay, or fine, expensive Hopi baskets.

A little more than one hundred miles south of the Navajo and Hopi reservations, the White Mountains rise above the surrounding plains and the Mogollon Rim. These gorgeous, forested mountains are a favorite vacation spot for city-dwellers from El Paso to Phoenix. The Apache-Sitgreaves National Forest, one of six national forests in Arizona, administers much of the area.

But a large block of the White Mountains became the Fort Apache Indian Reservation, occupied by the White Mountain Apache Tribe. The capital is at Whiteriver; historic Fort Apache, relinquished by the Army in 1924, is nearby.

White Mountain Apache clans provided General George Crook some of his fiercest enemies in the 1870s and 1880s, as well as some of his most loyal scouts.

In the 1950s, the Apaches began damming their fishing streams, creating dozens of small recreation lakes. The reservation became a magnet for southwestern trout fishermen. Here is found the only true native trout in Arizona, the Apache trout.

Later on, the Apaches built Sunrise, Arizona's largest and most successful ski resort. As non-Indian leases expired, the Apaches quietly let commercial lumber companies leave the reservation, and replaced the mills with Apache-owned mills. Few Anglos live on the reservation anymore, but with proper licenses from the tribe, they are always welcome to come and enjoy the tribe's share of the White Mountains.

Narrow, precipitous Havasu Canyon enters the Grand Canyon near its west end. You can't enter the canyon by automobile; you can only hike, or ride a rented horse. Supai Village at the bottom is the home of the Havasupai, one of several "pai" tribes that inhabit central and western Arizona—Yavapai, Hualapai, Havasupai.

Below the village, Havasu Creek goes over five spectacular waterfalls, including one 210 feet tall. Travertine carried in the water gives it an aquamarine cast, and forms exotic travertine pools.

This has long been recognized as Arizona's Shangri-la, a little heaven on earth. Naturalist Joseph Wood Krutch once wrote tongue-in-cheek of the Swiss resort which advertised, "Millions have come here seeking solitude." Oddly, it works for Supai. Cumulatively, millions have visited it, but the arduous trek in keeps crowds thin at any given time.

Arizona's varied natives don't lend themselves to pigeonholing, any more than does the varied society at large. Early in this century, Yaquis from Mexico fled revolutions and persecution, crossing an international border that was largely ceremonial at the time. They settled in villages in and around Phoenix, Tucson and Scottsdale. The federal government granted them a reservation near Tucson in the 1970's.

Yaquis have become integral parts of their communities, yet distinctive for their way of living. Their Easter observances, a blend of Christian ritual and such native rituals as the Deer Dance, have become part of the texture of Arizona culture.

You'll be welcomed by most Native Americans. Several tribes have tribal fairs, and larger reservations have visitor centers. Yavapais of the Verde Valley operate a visitor center on Interstate 17 at the Montezuma Castle turnoff, just north of Camp Verde. Pimas run a classy center on Interstate 10 about thirty miles south of Phoenix.

Don't be surprised if the Indians try to put you on a bit. It's a custom not much reported by anthropologists, and it stems from more than a century of erroneous perceptions and misplaced questions from whites.

Now and then we take a day-long jeep trip through Canyon de Chelly and Canyon del Muerto, a trip the young Navajo guides call "Shake-'N-Bake." In 1864, Kit Carson routed Navajos from these strongholds to start them on the notorious "Long Walk" to exile in New Mexico.

On our last jeep trip through Canyon de Chelly, the guide was Timothy, a young Navajo who had spent all of his 21 years in that area. Most of the people on such a trip are polite and sensitive, grateful to be enjoying the spectacular view and insight into native cultures. But there is always at least one pushy, impatient passenger. In this case, it was a couple.

The turnaround point for the fatiguing ride is Spider Rock, a sandstone needle reputed to be taller than the Washington Monument. It is said that Spider Woman lives atop the spire. Navajo children are warned that if they misbehave, Spider Woman will eat them.

As we rounded a bend in the canyon and the unmistakable spire came into view, the eager Anglo man brayed: "What's that?"

Timothy whirled and stared at Spider Rock, as though someone had put it there since his last visit.

"Gee, I don't know," he said.

SOUPS

Downtown Phoenix at dusk

Yogurt Spinach Soup

2 cups plain yogurt
1 (10 oz) pkg frozen, chopped spinach
¾ cup water
¾ cup Fresh Pic Cucumber Parsley Spinach Juice
1 tbsp chicken seasoned stock
½ tsp salt
½ tsp pepper
1 tbsp chopped dill
1 tbsp chopped chive
½ Sunkist® Lemon, sliced

• Put water, juice and stock in blender; add spinach, blend.
• Add remaining ingredients; blend thoroughly.
• Chill at least 1 hour before serving.
• Garnish with lemon slices.
• Serves 4.

Hearty Bean Soup

2 cups dried red kidney beans, rinsed
8 cups water
2½ cups chopped onion
6 carrots, cut into ½" thick slices
2 cups water
1 (12 oz) can tomato paste
1 tbsp Santa Cruz Chili Powder
1 tbsp salt
1½ tsp garlic salt
¼ tsp pepper
1¼ cups cubed UDA Seal of Arizona Provolone Cheese

• Cover beans with 8 cups water in large Dutch oven; bring to boil.
• Boil 2 minutes. Cover; let stand 1 hour.
• Uncover and bring to boil; cover.
• Simmer 45-50 minutes, or until beans are tender.
• Stir in vegetables, 2 cups water, tomato paste and seasonings; cover and simmer 30-35 minutes, or until carrots are tender.
• Stir cheese into hot soup just before serving.
• Makes 3 qts.

Cheddar Cheese Soup with Herbed Croutons

¼ cup UDA Seal of Arizona Butter
1 cup chopped celery
½ cup chopped onion
¼ cup all-purpose flour
1 tsp dry mustard
½ tsp salt
⅛ tsp pepper
3 cups Carnation® Milk
3 cups chicken broth
2 tsp Worcestershire sauce
4 cups shredded UDA Seal of Arizona Cheddar Cheese

Croutons:

8 slices Vienna bread, cut ½" thick
¼ cup UDA Seal of Arizona Butter
1 tbsp Italian seasoning

- Preheat oven to 400 degrees.
- For croutons, butter both sides of bread. Place on baking sheet and sprinkle with Italian seasoning.
- Bake until lightly browned, about 12 minutes; turn slices over and bake until browned, about 12 minutes longer.
- Cool; cut into cubes.
- For soup, melt butter in large Dutch oven.
- Sauté celery and onion until tender, about 10 minutes.
- Stir in flour and seasonings until smooth. Gradually add milk, broth and Worcestershire sauce.
- Bring to boiling, stirring constantly. Boil and stir 1 minute. Reduce heat to low.
- Gradually stir in cheese, stirring until cheese is melted after each addition.
- Serve with croutons.
- Serves 6.

Cheese Vegetable Chowder

2 cups chopped cabbage
1 cup onion slices
1 cup celery slices
1 cup frozen peas, thawed
1 cup thin carrot slices
½ cup UDA Seal of Arizona Butter
1 (16 oz) can cream style corn
2½ cups Foremost® Milk
1 tsp salt
⅛ tsp pepper
¼ tsp thyme
2½ cups shredded UDA Seal of Arizona
Sharp Cheddar Cheese

- Sauté cabbage, onion, celery, peas and carrots in butter in 3 qt saucepan 8-10 minutes, or until vegetables are tender, stirring frequently.
- Add corn, milk and seasonings; heat over low temperature 15 minutes, stirring occasionally.
- Add cheese, stir until melted.
- Makes 2 qts.

Creamy Italian Minestrone

2 (10.5 oz) cans condensed beef broth
1 (10 oz) pkg frozen, chopped spinach
1 (7 oz) pkg Creamettes® Elbow
Macaroni, uncooked
1 (10.75 oz) can cream tomato soup
1 (6 oz) can tomato paste
4 cups Shamrock® Milk
1½ cups sliced and quartered zucchini
1 tsp oregano
¼ tsp garlic powder
2 cups shredded UDA Seal of Arizona
Cheddar Cheese
½ cup grated Parmesan cheese
4 slices Beck's Bacon, cooked, drained
and crumbled

- Place beef broth and spinach in pot; cover and heat over low heat until spinach is thawed, about 10 minutes.
- Meanwhile, prepare macaroni according to pkg directions; drain.
- To pot add tomato soup and paste, milk, zucchini, oregano, garlic powder and macaroni.
- Bring to boil; reduce heat and simmer 10 minutes.
- Stir in Cheddar cheese until melted.
- Toss together Parmesan cheese and crumbled bacon. Serve as garnish on the soup.
- Makes 11 cups.

Cheesy Pumpkin Soup

2 tbsp UDA Seal of Arizona Butter
½ cup chopped green onion
2 tbsp all-purpose flour
1 tsp salt
½ tsp Sahuaro Spice Co. Nutmeg
¼ tsp Sahuaro Spice Co. Cinnamon
2½ cups milk
1 cup canned condensed chicken broth, undiluted
1 (16 oz) can pumpkin
1½ cups shredded UDA Seal of Arizona Muenster Cheese
sliced tomatoes
shredded UDA Seal of Arizona Muenster Cheese
chopped green onion

- Melt butter in heavy saucepan; add onion and sauté.
- Stir in flour, salt, nutmeg and cinnamon.
- Cook until smooth, stirring constantly. Remove from heat.
- Gradually stir in milk and chicken broth. Bring to boil over medium heat, stirring constantly.
- Add pumpkin, blending thoroughly.
- Simmer 5 minutes, stirring occasionally. Remove from heat.
- Add cheese, stirring until melted.
- Bring to serving temperature over low heat. Do not boil.
- Ladle into serving bowls and garnish with more cheese and chopped onion.
- Makes 6 cups.

Cheese Clam Chowder

2 cups diced, cooked potatoes
2 (7.5 oz) cans minced clams, undrained
1 (10.5 oz) can onion soup
1 (10.5 oz) can cream of celery soup
2 cups Foremost® Milk
1½ cups shredded UDA Seal of Arizona Cheddar Cheese
grated Parmesan cheese and chopped Rhee's Parsley to garnish

- Combine potatoes, clams and juice, onion and celery soups and milk in 3 qt saucepan; heat until simmering.
- Remove from heat and gradually add Cheddar cheese, blending well after each addition.
- If necessary, return to low heat to finish melting cheese, but do not boil.
- Serve garnished with Parmesan cheese and parsley.
- Makes 8 cups.

Chicken Corn Soup

1 (4 lb) Young's Farm Stewing Chicken

water

1 medium onion, chopped

2 stalks celery, diced

3 medium potatoes, cubed

1 small carrot, diced

¼ cup Fresh Touch Gardens Parsley

5 cups fresh or frozen Young's Farm Sweet Corn

2 tbsp sugar

3 hard boiled Laid In Arizona Eggs, sliced

salt and pepper

Dumplings:

1 cup all-purpose flour

1 Laid In Arizona Egg

¼ cup milk

- Cover chicken with water; cook until tender.
- Remove from water, cool, bone and cut into bite-size pieces; set aside.
- Strain stock; return to pot.
- Add onion, celery, potatoes, carrot, parsley, corn and sugar. Cook until vegetables are tender.
- Add chicken, hard boiled eggs, salt and pepper to taste
- For dumplings, blend flour, egg and milk together with 2 forks until crumbly. Drop into boiling soup; cover, simmer 5 minutes.
- Serves 8-10.

Gazpacho

6 large Pavo Tomatoes, chopped

¼ cup chopped Pavo Green Pepper

¼ cup chopped Pavo Sweet Red Pepper

2 medium Pavo Cucumbers, peeled, seeded and chopped

1 clove Rhee's Garlic, mashed

2 tbsp lemon juice

2 tbsp grated carrots

1½ tbsp grated onion

⅛ tsp Arizona Gunslinger Smokin' Hot Jalapeno Pepper Sauce

⅛ tsp oregano (optional)

3 tbsp French dressing

salt and pepper

- Mix all ingredients together.
- Chill before serving.
- Serves 4-6.

Spiced Shrimp Gazpacho

1 avocado, peeled, pitted and chopped	• Blend well all ingredients.
1 large onion, minced	• Chill overnight.
2 cloves garlic, minced	• Serve cold.
2 large Pavo Tomatoes, chopped	• Serves 6-8.
1 large Pavo Cucumber, peeled, seeded and chopped	
1 Pavo Green Bell Pepper, chopped	
3 tbsp olive oil	
3 tbsp red wine vinegar	
1 tsp basil	
2 tsp Mad Coyote Salsa Mix	
1 (48 oz) can tomato juice	
1 lb large shrimp, cooked and peeled	
⅓ cup fresh cilantro, chopped	

Chili Bueno

1 (16 oz) can pinto or black beans, drained	• Combine first 6 ingredients in large pot.
1 (16 oz) can kidney or red beans, drained	• In skillet, brown ground beef; drain.
1 (28 oz) can whole tomatoes	• Stir ground beef into bean mixture.
½ cup chopped green pepper (optional)	• Simmer 30 minutes to 1 hour.
½ cup chopped onions (optional)	• Serves 4-6.
1-1½ tbsp Mannons Chili Bueno	
1 lb Goldmark Lean Ground Beef	

Santa Cruz Valley Chili

2 lbs lean, coarse ground Arizona Beef
½ lb green bell peppers, diced
¾ lb onions, chopped
¼ cup minced parsley
2 (4 oz) jars Santa Cruz Chili Paste
1 tbsp salt
¾ tsp pepper
2½ tsp Santa Cruz Mexican Spice Mix
2 tbsp masa harina
2 tbsp water

- Brown ground beef in large pot over medium low heat.
- Add peppers and onions; cook until tender, stirring frequently.
- Add parsley and chili paste. Stir well; cook 10 minutes.
- Add salt, pepper and spice mix. Simmer, covered, over low heat 1 hour.
- Put masa harina into small bowl; add water. Mix into smooth paste.
- Add paste to chili; continue cooking, uncovered, 30 minutes.
- Skim off any fat before serving.
- Serves 6-8.

Guacamole Soup

2 ripe medium avocados
1½ cups water
1 cup milk
2 tbsp lemon juice
2½ tsp Sallie's Saltmix
1 tsp Arizona Smokin' Hot Jalepeno Pepper Sauce
1 medium tomato, chopped
Sunkist® Lemon Slices to garnish

- Cut avocados lengthwise into quarters; remove pits and peel.
- Mix avocado, water and milk in blender until smooth.
- Stir in lemon juice, seasoning salt and hot sauce thoroughly.
- Fold tomato into soup; chill.
- Garnish each serving with lemon slice.
- Serves 4-6.

Summer Fruit and Wine Soup

4 cups hulled fresh strawberries or raspberries, or both
½ cup R. W. Webb Johannisberg Riesling
1 cup Carnation® Smooth 'n' Creamy Plain Yogurt
1-2 cups water, chilled
¼-½ cup sugar

- Whirl berries in blender with wine.
- Strain to remove seeds, if desired.
- Return to blender with yogurt; add water and sugar, adjusting for desired consistency and sweetness.
- Chill at least 1 hour.
- Serve before meal as an appetizer or as light lunch.
- Serves 4.

Fresh Tomato Cucumber Soup

2 tbsp butter
¼ cup minced onion
2 cloves Rhee's Garlic, minced
3½ cups fresh tomato puree
2 (13.75 oz) cans chicken broth
1 cup Fresh Pic Cucumber Juice
¼ cup minced Rhee's Parsley
½ cup minced Rhee's Basil
fresh basil and cooked shrimp to garnish

- In large stock pot or saucepan, heat butter over medium heat to melt.
- Add onion and garlic; sauté until soft.
- Add tomato puree, broth, cucumber juice and herbs; mix well.
- Bring mixture to boil; reduce heat and simmer 45 minutes.
- Chill or serve hot.
- Garnish each serving with fresh basil and shrimp.
- Serves 4-6.

Sausage Soup

1 (14.75 oz) can chicken broth
1 (15.25 oz) can Great Northern or other white beans, drained
¾ cup water
½ cup uncooked Creamette® Rigatoni
1 cup sliced Goldmark Polish Sausage
1 bay leaf
1 tbsp onion flakes
1 tsp parsley flakes

- Combine all ingredients in saucepan.
- Bring to boil; simmer 10 minutes.
- Serves 4.

Minted Summer Squash Soup

1 cup Foremost® Half & Half

½ cup packed Fresh Touch Gardens Mint Leaves

¼ cup butter

¾ cup sliced Copperhead Green Onions

½ cup shredded carrot

1 clove Fresh Touch Gardens Garlic, minced

5 cups sliced mixed summer squash (yellow and zucchini)

3 cups condensed chicken broth

salt and pepper

- Place cream and mint in blender container; cover.
- Puree until smooth; set aside.
- Melt butter in large saucepan.
- Sauté onions, carrot and garlic until tender, about 5 minutes.
- Add squash and broth.
- Heat to boiling. Simmer, covered, 10-12 minutes, or until squash is tender.
- Place ⅓ squash mixture in blender container; cover. Puree until smooth.
- Repeat with remaining squash mixture.
- Return puree to saucepan.
- Season to taste with salt and pepper.
- Heat thoroughly, but do not boil.
- Stir in reserved cream mixture.
- Serve immediately.
- Serves 4-6.

Spinach Curry Soup

1½ lbs Copperhead Spinach Leaves

3 cups water

2½ tbsp Sahuaro Spice Co. Curry Paste

1 tbsp Shamrock® Whipping Cream or Sour Cream

1 cup Shamrock® Milk (optional)

grated Parmesan cheese

freshly ground pepper

- Wash spinach thoroughly so that no sand remains. Place spinach in saucepan; add water. Bring to boil.
- Turn off heat; let cool 10 minutes.
- Puree boiled spinach in blender.
- Add curry paste to puree; reheat to serving temperature.
- Turn off heat; add whipping or sour cream and milk, if necessary.
- Sprinkle on cheese, add pepper to taste and serve hot.
- Serves 4.

PICANTE Y CALIENTE

"When I was a kid, the little Mexican boys came around door-to-door, selling tamales out of a bucket. There was nothing like it."
—A frequently-uttered remembrance of Arizona natives.

Although Arizonans grow increasingly worldly about food, there is no stronger ethnic influence here than that of Mexico. It was true in territorial days, and it is true today.

Early U.S. visitors to Prescott, the first territorial capital, noted with pride that it was an "American" town, compared to raffish Tucson with its ground-hugging, adobe feel of Mexico. But the Juniper House, Prescott's first hotel, opened in 1864 with a dining room menu that relied heavily on chili dishes.

Mexicans who lived in the region before the Treaty of Guadalupe Hidalgo and the Gadsden Purchase were offered automatic U.S. citizenship, and many accepted it. Others migrated northward in increasing numbers.

They farmed, ranched, manned the state's mines and commercial establishments. They were freighters, statesmen, teachers, musicians,

laborers and capitalists.

They were Sonorans, mostly, but a number of people with roots in Chihuahua came into northern and eastern parts of the state through New Mexico. The migration continues today. Many Arizona families are branches of families in Sonora—or vice versa.

Please permit me to write personally about Mexican food, because it is such a personal thing to so many Arizonans. Frequently, preferences in Mexican flavors divide spouses, siblings, generations in the same family. The end product of this good-natured warfare is a constant quest for the "best" Mexican food.

I seek flavors and textures remembered from my unsophisticated youth in the lumbering town of Flagstaff, where Hispanic women ran little restaurants in their homes. My wife seeks the kind of Mexican food she remembers from the ranch country around Springerville. Others seek the flavors remembered from forgotten mining towns.

Traditional Mexican cooking in northern Arizona differs from that south of the Gila River; the same dish may have a different flavor and a different name in various regions of the state.

And visitors and newcomers sample the wares of an intimidating range of Mexican food restaurants, trying to establish their own preferences. Arizona's Mexican food restaurants are influenced by Sonora, by Chihuahua, by Tex-Mex, by California.

Arizona lately has been a test tube for innovative restaurateurs who use the humble flour tortilla to dress tasty, lighter concoctions. As for the traditional, easy combination plate, many chefs seem to be competing to see who can use the most *cumino*, not always popular with traditionalists who like the flavor of the chilis (and the enhancing garlic) to dominate.

Ultimately, many Arizonans cook their own Mexican dishes, perhaps the most satisfying solution to what could otherwise be a lifetime dilemma.

This is not about contest-grade red chili con carne, the circus dish

Ted De Grazia's "Gallery of the Sun" near Tucson

51

favored by promoters, U.S. senators and chauvinists everywhere, a boon to the growers of *cumino* and tomatoes. I wrote as much balderdash about that kind of chili as any southwestern writer.

But a few years back, I actually learned to cook chili. My wife said that encouraging me to cook was the only way she could approach the remembered flavors of her childhood. For myself, I try to recapture elusive flavors which the odd Hispanic sheepherder or wood chopper has shared with me during my years as a journalist.

Now I let my chilis speak for themselves: a modest red called "World War III", and a deceptively delicate green called "Chili Verde Verdad"— true green chili. There are two Spanish words for "hot"—*picante* for piquancy, *caliente* for temperature. Technically, *caliente* ought to mean stovetop temperature. But I prefer to think of *picante* as the distinctive bite of chili, and *caliente* as its innate fire, the smoldering aftertaste. My green chili is of a delayed-action variety which allows your palate to savor the delicate *picante* before the *caliente* kicks in and sets out to rid your system of its poisons.

Despite its show-biz reputation, red chili con carne, also called picadillo, is an essential ingredient of many Mexican dishes.

Frequently, the second step in a newcomer's initiation to Mexican food is *machaca*, a form of carne *seca*, a dried, shredded beef—jerky, in other words, frequently more heavily spiced than its gringo counterpart. It originated for the same reason as jerky—a lack of ice and refrigeration on the frontier. *Machaca* is served in many ways—with vegetables in a sort of hash, and in burros and enchiladas.

Chili rellenos remain essentially simple, and hot. The lowly bean burro—refried beans in a flour tortilla wrapper—has graduated to include a number of ingredients, stopping just short of peanut butter.

The word "enchilada" covers a lot of territory: cheese enchiladas, with and without onions; green or red meat enchiladas, and so on. These creations usually are wrapped in flour tortillas, but do you know about stacked enchiladas? A loose red chili con carne mixture, the consistency of spaghetti sauce, is layered between oil-softened corn tortillas—one layer, two layers, three layers. The masterpiece is garnished with any or all of the usual toppings: grated cheese, lettuce, tomatoes, onions.

And crowned with a fried egg. Or two. Maybe some of the sauce from the chili mixture spooned over the top, eh?

Relatives exiled to careers in the East are not too picky when they fly home for a visit—any old Mexican food will serve the deprived palate. But the exiles will make a special trip home for stacked enchiladas.

The *chimichanga* is apparently a gringo dish, a gift-wrapped meat burro topped with sour cream and guacamole. But if chefs in interior Mexico have not adopted it, they are missing a bet.

The author's personal quest includes looking for a good bowl of *albondigas* soup—meatball soup, usually heavy on the cilantro and sometimes with red chili. Hispanics relish menudo, a soup that includes tripe, hominy and, again, cilantro. It is a legendary cure for hangovers.

One New Year's Day team ropers from the Globe-Miami mining region gathered for a competition near Wheatfields. The hosts and many participants were Hispanic, and some wore heads that were *muy crudo* from New Year's Eve libations.

All morning long they cried out, "Is the menudo ready yet?" Their agility and their accuracy with lariats improved markedly around noon, after the menudo had been dished up.

Obviously we're only hitting the unsophisticated high spots here. There is an enormous range of more complex Mexican entrees, accompaniments, appetizers and desserts.

Traditionalists who seek "purity" in Mexican food may be chasing phantoms. From what I have been able to read, Hispanics in Arizona used whatever ingredients were available; the traditional dishes were vehicles for these ingredients.

Anglo dinner tables frequently included a bowl of *frijoles* (pinto beans) as a side dish, and a bowl of red chili con carne to be used as an accompaniment or a condiment. Green chilies were used to accent many varieties of salad and casserole.

Tamales date back to the Aztecs. The basic tamale—red chili meat wrapped in *masa* and corn husks, remains a staple in the Southwest, as well as a traditional Christmas Eve dish or gift. Some Hispanic and Anglo women spend an illogical amount of time making tamales; it is almost a religious exercise.

My father used to talk nostalgically of trading his sandwiches to Hispanic kids for tamales when he was in grade school near Peoria in the 1920s. Nearly every town had young, door-to-door tamale vendors, dispensing tamales from lard buckets.

Today I sometimes buy tamales on the streets of downtown Phoenix. The woman who makes and sells them has replaced the traditional lard bucket with a large, blue plastic pail. Her tamales are bundled six to a foil-wrapped package, five dollars for half a dozen.

But inside the foil, inside the corn husk, the tamales remain the same, my link with the savory memories of childhood.

SALADS

Roundup in Monument Valley

Honeyed Ambrosia

4 medium Sunkist® Oranges

1 medium banana

½ cup orange juice

¼ cup Mountain Top Honey

2 tbsp lemon juice

¼ cup flaked coconut

- Pare oranges; cut crosswise into thin slices; place into serving bowl.
- Peel banana; cut thin slices into bowl with oranges. Toss fruits.
- Blend orange juice, honey and lemon juice; pour over fruits. Sprinkle with coconut.
- Serves 4-6.

Arizona Grape Salad Supreme

¼ cup cooked crisp, chopped Beck's Bacon

1 head Romaine lettuce, rinsed and torn

1 head butterleaf lettuce, rinsed and torn

½ head escarole, rinsed and torn

2 lbs seedless grapes

¼ (750 ml) btl Arizona Vineyards Workers Red

1 tbsp stone ground mustard

2 limes, juiced

4 tbsp Crockett's Honey

1 tbsp coarse ground pepper

1 tsp rosemary

2 tbsp chopped Fresh Touch Gardens Basil

⅓ cup olive oil

wine vinegar to taste

1 tsp salt

garlic to taste

pecans (optional)

- In large bowl, combine all lettuce and grapes; set aside.
- To make dressing, mix well next 11 ingredients; pour over salad and toss.
- Top with pecans.
- Serves 8-12.

Honeyed Grapefruit Salad

2 Sunkist® Grapefruits, sectioned

2 Sunkist® Oranges, sectioned

1 pt strawberries, washed and hulled

2 medium avocados, peeled, pitted and sliced

1 banana, peeled and sliced

½ Copperhead Cantaloupe or Honeydew Melon, peeled and cut into bite-size pieces

Dressing:

⅔ cup vegetable oil

1 tsp freshly grated grapefruit peel

⅓ cup freshly squeezed Sunkist® Grapefruit Juice

2 tbsp freshly squeezed Sunkist® Lemon Juice

2 tbsp Malcom's Honey

½ tsp paprika

½ tsp salt

- To make dressing, combine all ingredients in jar with lid; chill.
- Arrange fruit in large salad bowl or on individual salad plates.
- Shake chilled salad dressing vigorously; pour on salad before serving.
- Serves 4-6.

Fresh Tangerine Cole Slaw

3 Sunkist® Tangerines

¼ cup vegetable oil

grated peel of ½ Sunkist® Tangerine

1 Sunkist® Tangerine, juiced

½ Sunkist® Lemon, juiced

2 tbsp Mountain Top Honey

1 tbsp toasted sesame seeds (optional)

1 small head cabbage, cut in long thin shreds

½ cup raisins

¼ cup chopped Wold's Peanuts

- Peel and section tangerines. Cut sections in half and remove seeds.
- In jar with lid, combine oil, tangerine peel and juice, lemon juice, honey and sesame seeds; shake well.
- In large bowl, combine cabbage, tangerines, raisins and dressing; chill.
- To serve, add chopped nuts; toss gently.
- Serves 6.

Pistachios and Fruit

3 Sunkist® Oranges
1 tbsp packed brown sugar
2 tsp lemon juice
¼ tsp cinnamon
2 Brown's Pears, cored, sliced and
dipped in lemon juice
¾ cup red seedless grapes
¼ cup chopped Triple A Pistachios

- Squeeze juice from 1 orange; peel remaining oranges and slice crosswise.
- Combine orange juice, sugar, lemon juice and cinnamon; pour over oranges, pears and grapes. Chill at least 2 hours.
- Sprinkle with pistachios just before serving.
- Serves 6.

Pineapple Waldorf Salad

2 Valley's Finest Red Delicious Apples
2 Valley's Finest Golden Delicious Apples
1 cup coarsely chopped celery
1 (13 oz or larger) can pineapple
chunks, drained (reserve syrup
for dressing)
lettuce leaves
½ cup slivered, roasted almonds
(optional)

Dressing:
2 Laid In Arizona Eggs
¼ cup pineapple juice
2 tbsp lemon juice
¼ cup sugar
½ cup sour cream

- To make dressing, beat eggs until light; add juices and sugar.
- Cook and stir constantly until thick.
- Stir in sour cream; set aside.
- Leave skin on apples; core and chop. Mix apples, celery and pineapple.
- Add dressing to apples; stir well.
- Line glass bowl with lettuce leaves; pour in salad. Chill well.
- Before serving, sprinkle almonds on top, if desired.
- Serves 4-6.

7 Layer Salad

1 small head lettuce, shredded
½ cup sliced celery
⅓ cup sliced green onion
1 (10 oz) pkg frozen peas
2 cups mayonnaise
½ cup grated UDA Seal of Arizona Cheddar Cheese
6 slices Beck's Bacon, cooked and crumbled

- Layer lettuce, celery, onion and peas in bowl.
- Spread mayonnaise completely on top, to sides of bowl.
- Cover with plastic wrap; let stand in refrigerator at least 6 hours, or overnight.
- Just before serving, sprinkle cheese and bacon over salad.
- Serves 6-8.

Fancy Cabbage

1 medium Pavo Green Bell Pepper, chopped
2 cups thickly sliced celery
1 medium Copperhead Onion, chopped
3 tbsp margarine
1 tsp sugar
1 (8 oz) can tomato sauce
1 head cabbage, shredded
salt and pepper

- In large skillet, sauté bell pepper, celery and onion in margarine.
- Stir in sugar, tomato sauce, cabbage, salt and pepper to taste.
- Simmer until cabbage is tender, about 12 minutes.
- Serves 4-6.

Hot Cabbage Slaw

2 tbsp vegetable oil
1 tsp Sahuaro Spice Co. Salt
½ tsp Sahuaro Spice Co. Celery Seed
1 lb cabbage, shredded
½ tsp sugar
dash Sahuaro Spice Co. Pepper
2 tbsp vinegar

- Heat oil in skillet.
- Add all ingredients except vinegar.
- Cover; cook over medium heat 3 minutes, stirring occasionally.
- Add vinegar, stir and serve hot.
- Serves 4.

Cauliflower Salad Bowl

4 cups thinly sliced raw
Copperhead Cauliflower

1 cup very coarsely chopped pitted
ripe olives

⅔ cup coarsely chopped green pepper

½ cup coarsely chopped pimento

½ cup chopped Copperhead Onion

lettuce leaves

Dressing:

½ cup vegetable oil

3 tbsp lemon juice

3 tbsp wine vinegar

2 tsp sage

½ tsp sugar

¼ tsp Santa Cruz Pepper

- In medium bowl, combine cauliflower, olives, green pepper, pimento and onion.
- Make dressing by combining all ingredients in small bowl and beating with rotary beater until well blended. Pour over cauliflower mixture.
- Refrigerate, covered, until well chilled, 4 hours to overnight.
- To serve, spoon salad into bowl lined with lettuce leaves. Toss just before serving.
- Serves 4-6.

Copper Pennies

2 lbs carrots, sliced

1 Pavo Green Pepper, chopped

1 onion, chopped

½ cup sliced celery

Dressing:

½ (10.75 oz) can tomato soup

⅜ cup sugar

½ tsp Arizona Champagne
Mustard Sauce

½ tsp Worcestershire sauce

¼ cup vegetable oil

⅜ cup vinegar

salt and pepper

- Boil sliced carrots until just tender; drain well.
- Cool; add green pepper, onion and celery.
- For dressing, thoroughly blend all ingredients in blender; refrigerate.
- Toss together vegetables and dressing.
- Serves 8-12.

Shrimp Pasta Salad

1 (14 oz) pkg De Cio Pasta Beet, Carrot
or Sweet Green Pea Conchiglia, cooked
½ red bell pepper, sliced
1 stalk celery, chopped
½ lb shrimp, deveined, cooked and cut
in chunks
1 (6 oz) can water chestnuts, sliced
salt and pepper

Dressing:
1 cup mayonnaise
1 tbsp Arizona Champagne
Mustard Sauce
1 tbsp brown sugar
1 tbsp fresh lemon juice
3 heaping tbsp Foremost® Sour Cream

- Mix dressing ingredients well; chill.
- Rinse cooked conchiglia with cold water; drain.
- In a large bowl, add pepper, celery and shrimp; toss well.
- Pour dressing on mixture; toss well.
- Add salt and pepper to taste.
- Refrigerate 1 hour before serving.
- Serves 4-6.

Pistachio Turkey Salad

3 cups shredded, cooked Young's Farm
Turkey or Chicken
1 cup seedless green grapes, halved
1 small green onion, chopped
¾ cup Triple A Pistachios, lightly
toasted, divided
2 tbsp mayonnaise
2 tbsp Carnation® Sour Cream
2 tsp lemon juice
¾ tsp minced fresh dill or tarragon
salt and pepper
salad greens

- In a medium mixing bowl, combine turkey or chicken, grapes, green onion and ½ cup pistachios.
- Coarsely chop remaining pistachios; set aside.
- In a small mixing bowl, stir together mayonnaise, sour cream, lemon juice, dill or tarragon.
- Fold mayonnaise mixture into turkey mixture.
- Season with salt and pepper to taste.
- Serve on salad greens. Sprinkle with chopped pistachios.
- Serves 4-6.

Raw Vegetable Salad

1 bunch Copperhead Broccoli
1 bunch Copperhead Green Onions
2 Pavo Green Peppers
1 head Copperhead Cauliflower
1 lb carrots
1 pt Pavo Cherry Tomatoes, halved
1 pkg Italian dressing mix
1 (8 oz) btl Italian dressing

- Cut vegetables into small pieces; place in large bowl.
- Sprinkle dressing mix on top; refrigerate overnight.
- Before serving, add Italian dressing; stir well.
- Serves 8-10.

Pistachio Macaroni Salad

½ (1 lb) pkg Creamette® Rotini, uncooked
2 cups torn fresh Copperhead Spinach
1 cup chopped tomato
1 cup blanched pea pods
¼ cup chopped Arizona Nuts Pistachios
pepper
grated Parmesan cheese

Oregano Dressing:
¼ cup vegetable oil
¼ cup red wine vinegar
¾ tsp crushed oregano
⅛ tsp garlic powder

- Combine dressing ingredients; set aside.
- Prepare rotini according to pkg directions; drain.
- Marinate hot rotini in dressing; cool to room temperature.
- Combine with spinach, tomato, pea pods, pistachios and pepper to taste.
- Sprinkle with Parmesan cheese.
- Serves 8.

Cowboy Style Antipasto Salad

1 cup halved Pavo Cherry Tomatoes

1 cup sliced black olives

1 cup sliced mushrooms

1 large Pavo Green Bell Pepper, julienned

1 large Pavo Sweet Red Pepper, julienned

1 large Pavo Yellow Bell Pepper, julienned

4 oz Monterey Jack cheese, cut into strips

4 oz Cowboy Cheese, cut into strips

8 oz Cowboy Quiltie Salami, cut into strips

Dressing:

1/4 cup vinegar

1/3 cup olive oil or vegetable oil

1/4 cup water

2 tbsp sugar

1 (3 oz) pkg Authentic Cowboy Salsa Seasoning

- Mix all dressing ingredients together; let stand 10 minutes.
- Pour dressing over combined vegetables.
- Cover; marinate in refrigerator.
- Drain; arrange vegetables on platter.
- Serve with reserved marinade.
- Serves 6-8.

Marinated Beef Salad

3/4 cup Miguel's Medium Salsa

3 tbsp vegetable oil

2 tbsp red wine vinegar

1/2 cup minced red onion

1/2 lb Arizona Beef Roast, cooked, sliced into strips

lettuce

1 tomato, cut in wedges

1/2 cup ripe olives, sliced

1 avocado, peeled, pitted and sliced

- Combine salsa, oil, vinegar and onion in bowl.
- Add roast beef; stir to coat with mixture.
- Cover; refrigerate at least 1 hour.
- Serve on lettuce garnished with tomato wedges, olives and sliced avocado.
- Serves 3-4.

Auntie's Pasta Salad

2-3 cups water

1 lb fresh mushrooms, washed and sliced

lemon juice

1 (14 oz) pkg De Cio Pasta Tomato, Spinach or Carrot Conchiglia, cooked, rinsed and drained

salt and pepper

1 (6 oz) can black olives, sliced

1 (5 oz) jar green stuffed olives, sliced

Dressing:

½ cup olive oil

½ cup red wine vinegar

1 tsp Sahuaro Spice Co. Oregano, or to taste

- Mix dressing ingredients in shaker; chill.
- In medium saucepan, let water come to boil. Put in mushrooms; return to full, rolling boil; drain and place in bowl.
- Add lemon juice to half-cover mushrooms, stirring to coat.
- Place conchiglia in second bowl. Add salt and pepper to taste; add olives.
- Drain mushrooms; add to mixture.
- Pour on well shaken dressing. Toss together; chill.
- Serves 4-6.

Mexican Barley Salad

1 (14 oz) pkg Territorial Gourmet Mexican Barley Stew Mix

2 cloves Fresh Touch Gardens Garlic, minced

2 tbsp olive oil

1 (4 oz) jar Territorial Gourmet Olé Pasta Sauce

10 cups hot water

½ cup Salsa De Las Catalinas Verde

¼ cup diced fresh cilantro

- Cook barley mix according to pkg directions, omitting meat.
- In large soup pan, sauté garlic in olive oil.
- Add pasta sauce instead of chopped canned tomatoes.
- Add barley mix and water to sauce.
- Cook according to directions, adding additional water if necessary.
- Add salsa to hot, cooked barley.
- Cover and chill at least 4 hours.
- Garnish with cilantro.
- Serves 6-8.

Warm Goat Cheese and Pistachios

11 oz goat cheese
1 cup chopped Arizona Nuts Pistachios
¼ cup olive oil
16 slices baguette, toasted
strawberry slices and watercress to garnish

Sauce:
4 egg yolks
1 egg
4 tbsp pear vinegar
1 lemon, juiced
3 cloves Rhee's Garlic, minced
½ cup chopped Rhee's Basil
2 cups peanut oil
salt and pepper

- Slice goat cheese into 4, ¾" thick patties.
- Put 1 slice of cheese at a time in bowl with pistachios, pressing down firmly to fully encrust cheese. Take from bowl and set aside.
- To make sauce, place egg yolks and egg in blender.
- Add vinegar, lemon juice, garlic and fresh basil. Blend until smooth; slowly add oil until desired consistency. Salt and pepper to taste.
- In 8" non-stick skillet over medium heat, add olive oil. When oil is hot, place goat cheese slices in pan.
- Cook both sides until nuts are toasted; remove from skillet; place on warm salad plate.
- Place 1 spoonful of sauce in middle of plate; place goat cheese on top of sauce.
- Garnish plate with toast, strawberry slices and watercress.
- Serves 4.

Chicken-Rotini Salad

½ (1 lb) pkg Creamette® Rotini or Rotelle, uncooked
3 cups chopped, cooked Young's Farm Chicken
1½ cups sliced celery
1 medium red bell pepper, chopped
1 cup frozen peas, cooked and drained
¼ cup sliced Arnold's Green Olives
¼ cup sliced green onions
¾ cup bottled Italian dressing
¼ cup grated Parmesan cheese
¼ tsp pepper

- Prepare rotini according to pkg directions; drain.
- In medium bowl, combine rotini and remaining ingredients; mix well.
- Cover; chill thoroughly.
- Toss gently before serving.
- Serves 6-8.

Curried Chicken Salad

2½ cups diced, cooked chicken
1 cup cubed pineapple, papaya or
seedless grapes
1 cup diced celery
½ cup diced water chestnuts
1 tsp curry powder
1 tbsp Cinnabar Asian Tamarind Sauce
½ cup mayonnaise
¼ cup Foremost® Sour Cream
¼ cup Sallie's Indian Mango or Ceylon
Pineapple Ginger Chutney
1 tbsp lemon juice
1 head lettuce, shredded
½ cup slivered, toasted almonds

- Mix chicken with fruit, celery and water chestnuts.
- Dissolve curry powder in tamarind sauce; combine with mayonnaise, sour cream, chutney and lemon juice.
- Mix chicken with dressing.
- Serve on lettuce; sprinkle with almonds.
- Serves 4-5.

Desert Chicken Salad

1 (3.5 oz) can chicken
½ cup raisins
¼ cup Shamrock® Sour Cream
¼ cup mayonnaise
3 slices pineapple, chopped
¼ cup Cahill Desert Products
Pomegranate Jelly
sliced fruit to garnish
assorted crackers

- Combine all ingredients in mixing bowl; stir thoroughly.
- Serve with crackers.
- Serves 2-4.

SAUCES

*St. Mary's Basilica—a historic backdrop for one of
Phoenix' modern sculptures*

Orange Pecan Glaze

⅓ cup concentrated orange juice
3 tbsp Country Estate Pecan Meal
1 tbsp brown sugar

- Mix together all ingredients.
- Baste ham, chicken or fish with glaze several times while cooking.
- Makes ⅔ cup.

Barbecue Sauce

¼ cup Arizona Champagne Mustard Sauce
¼ cup Arizona Champagne Jalapeno Jelly
¼ cup vinegar
½ cup molasses

- Mix together all ingredients.
- Simmer 10-15 minutes.
- Use as glaze on all barbecue foods.
- Makes 1¼ cups.

Jalapeno Marinade

1 cup Cheri's Jalapeno Jelly
1½ cups water
¼ cup red wine vinegar
2 tsp dried sweet basil
½-1 tsp black pepper
⅓ cup olive oil

- Combine jalapeno jelly and water; heat until jelly dissolves; cool.
- Add remaining ingredients; shake until thoroughly mixed.
- Immerse chicken in marinade 1 hour at room temperature, or 3-4 hours in refrigerator.
- Barbecue or broil chicken, adding additional marinade while cooking.
- Makes 2 cups.

Wild Orange Ham Glaze

⅓ cup Saguaro Honey
2 tbsp brown sugar
⅓ cup Cahill Desert Products Wild Orange Marmalade
1 tsp Sallie's Saltmix
1 tsp yellow mustard
1 (10-12 lb) Beck's Mesquite Bone-In Ham

- Combine all ingredients in saucepan; heat slowly.
- Stir constantly until sauce is smooth and pourable.
- Place ham in oven; continually baste with mixture until cooked, 3-3½ hours.
- After slicing, pour extra glaze over each slice.
- Serves 12-14.

Honey Sweet and Sour Sauce

1 (16 oz) can tomatoes, chopped
1 (8 oz) can crushed pineapple
1 cup Mountain Top Honey
½ cup red wine vinegar
1 tbsp soy sauce
1 tsp ginger
½ tsp salt (optional)
½ cup chopped Copperhead Onion
1 Pavo Green Bell Pepper, cut into ½" slices
2 tbsp cornstarch
3 tbsp cold water

- Put tomatoes and pineapple in a heavy saucepan.
- Heat on low; gradually stir in honey.
- Add vinegar, soy sauce, ginger and salt.
- Add onion and green pepper. Simmer uncovered, 20 minutes, stirring constantly to prevent scorching.
- Stir cornstarch into water; add to sauce slowly. Simmer until thickened.
- Store in refrigerator.
- Honey content may cause crystallization; heat to melt.
- Excellent with pork chops, ribs or chicken, or over cooked rice.
- Makes 5 cups.

Santa Cruz Enchilada Sauce

1 tbsp all-purpose flour
1 tbsp oil
1 (15 oz) jar Santa Cruz Chili & Spice Chili Paste
3-4 cups hot water or beef or chicken broth
2 tbsp garlic powder
¼ tsp cumin
1 tsp Santa Cruz Chili & Spice Oregano

- Combine all ingredients in a saucepan; simmer gently 15 minutes.
- Makes 6 cups.

Note:
For thicker sauce use less liquid.

Arizona Chili Sauce

2 tbsp shortening
2 tbsp all-purpose flour
¼ cup Sahuaro Spice Co. Chili Powder
2 cups chicken or beef bouillon, or water
3 tsp salt
1 tsp Sahuaro Spice Co. Garlic Powder
½ tsp Sahuaro Spice Co. Oregano
½ tsp Sahuaro Spice Co. Coriander
¼ tsp Sahuaro Spice Co. Cumin

- Heat shortening in saucepan.
- Stir in flour; cook for 1 minute.
- Add chili powder and ½ cup bouillon or water; cook for 1 minute.
- Add remaining seasonings and liquid; simmer for 10 minutes.
- Makes 2 cups.

Mystery Spaghetti Sauce

1 (16 oz) jar Marinara Spaghetti Sauce
½ cup Desert Rose Medium Red Salsa

- Combine ingredients.
- Heat in saucepan.
- Makes 2½ cups.

Red Rock Crossing, Oak Creek

Cajun Spice

1 tbsp Sahuaro Spice Co. Cayenne

1 tbsp Sahuaro Spice Co. Garlic Salt

2 tsp Sahuaro Spice Co. Dried Basil

1½ tsp crushed Sahuaro Spice Co.
Bay Leaves

1½ tsp Sahuaro Spice Co. Crushed
Black Pepper

1 tsp Sahuaro Spice Co. White Pepper

1 tsp Sahuaro Spice Co. Sage

1 tsp Sahuaro Spice Co. Thyme

½ tsp Sahuaro Spice Co. Allspice

- Put ingredients in blender; blend until whole bay leaves are ground fine.

- Makes about 5 tbsp.

Homemade Curry Powder

2 tbsp Sahuaro Spice Co. Coriander

2 tbsp Sahuaro Spice Co. Cumin

1 tbsp Sahuaro Spice Co. Mace

2 tsp Sahuaro Spice Co. Cardamon

2 tsp Sahuaro Spice Co. Cinnamon

1 tsp Sahuaro Spice Co. Cloves

1 tsp Sahuaro Spice Co. Nutmeg

1 tsp Sahuaro Spice Co. Tumeric

1 tsp Sahuaro Spice Co. Coarse
Black Pepper

½ tsp Sahuaro Spice Co. Cayenne

- Mix spices together; store in airtight container.

- Makes about 6 tbsp.

Pistachio Mayonnaise

½ cup Triple A Pistachios
1½ cups olive or corn oil
½ cup extra virgin olive oil
3 large egg yolks
1 lemon, juiced
salt and white pepper

- Roast pistachios at 325 degrees 5 minutes and finely chop.
- Combine oils.
- Place yolks with lemon juice in food processor.
- With mixer going, drizzle in oil until mayonnaise forms.
- Remove from bowl.
- Salt and pepper to taste.
- Add chopped pistachios.
- Makes 2½ cups.

Peach or Apricot Jam

6 cups chopped peaches or apricots
1 box powdered pectin
2½ cups Mountain Top Honey
¼ cup lemon juice
paraffin

- Place fruit in large saucepan. Mash and heat slowly.
- As juice increases turn up heat and cook 15 minutes.
- Add pectin, stirring well.
- Bring to boil; add honey and lemon juice, stirring well.
- Heat rapidly to full rolling boil.
- Cook for 5 minutes.
- Melt paraffin.
- Spoon hot into jars to within ½" of top. Pour paraffin to top of jar.
- Process in boiling water bath 10 minutes.
- Makes 6 half pints.

Raita

1 cup plain nonfat yogurt
1 medium Pavo Cucumber, peeled,
  seeded and thinly sliced
1 tsp minced fresh ginger
salt

- Mix together all ingredients.
- Chill before serving.
- Serve as accompaniment with spicy main dishes.
- Makes 1½-2 cups.

Herb Blend Pesto

2 large cloves Fresh Touch
  Gardens Garlic
1 cup Fresh Touch Gardens Basil
½ cup Fresh Touch Gardens Oregano
¼ cup Fresh Touch Gardens Savory
¼ cup Fresh Touch Gardens
  Sweet Marjoram
¼ cup pine nuts
½ cup grated Romano cheese
½ cup olive oil

- In food processor or blender chop garlic and herbs.
- Add nuts and cheese; chop again.
- While chopping, drizzle in oil.
- Let stand 10-15 minutes before serving.
- Can be stored in refrigerator 2-3 weeks, or frozen 6 months or longer.
- Makes 2 cups.

Spaghetti Sauce

2 lbs Barone Italian Sausage, hot or mild
½ cup chopped onions
2 cloves Rhee's Garlic
½ cup Rhee's Parsley
2 (29 oz) cans tomatoes
2 (4 oz) cans tomato paste
½ cup sugar
4 tsp salt
1½ tsp basil
2 tsp oregano
½ tsp garlic powder

- Brown sausage; add onions, garlic and parsley; saute.
- Blend or chop tomatoes; combine with tomato paste and remaining ingredients.
- Add to sausage and onions; simmer 1½-2 hours.
- Makes 6 cups.

GOLD, GHOSTS AND MELTING POTS

"This territory is rich in minerals, probably by developing will prove to be the richest in the world. Gold, silver and copper are to be found upon prospecting, in all sections of the country."
                    —Jonathan Richmond, letter from Tucson, 1864.

Some of the earliest and most dedicated miners drawn to Arizona were "Cousin Jacks," Cornish miners who considered their work a craft. They carried into the underground mines lunchboxes stocked with "pasties," meat pie filling baked into a turnover. Pasties were portable, clean and handy to eat at mid-shift.

The miners from Cornwall carried something else into the mines, despite themselves. Tommyknockers, invisible sprites, stowed away in the lunchboxes. In the mines they tapped and knocked and creaked, showing the miners where the good ore lay, warning of cave-ins, talking to the Cousin Jacks of life-and-death matters.

There are a lot of sprites and ghosts and spirits in Arizona's mines and mining towns. Ghosts, mostly, for a mining town is born to die as soon as the ore plays out. Maps and record books and old newspapers tell of hundreds of towns that existed for a few weeks or a few years, then vanished:

Fool's Gulch, McMillanville, Christmas, La Paz, Gila City, Providence, Huron, Stanton, Weaver, Octave, Poland.

Total Wreck, Helvetia, Bellevue, Gleeson, Signal, Swansea, Quijotoa, Gillett, Goodwin, Crown King, Harqua Hala, Mascot, Chloride, Goldroad.

Not to imply that Arizona's mining industry is dead. Despite an almost constant reshaping, it thrives, employing several thousand workers. Some of the live mining towns are still repositories for a lot of folklore.

As for the dear departed places, you can still find remnants of many of the towns. And a few of the old ghosts are downright healthy—hauntingly so, you might say. People make a big deal of Halloween in Jerome, the state's liveliest ghost town, and in Bisbee, which never died; it just switched occupations.

In mining towns they tell of La Llorona, the weeping woman, Arizona's best-known ghost. She was an immoral woman. Some versions say she was a poor, working-class girl who fell in love with a rich lover; he spurned her and married into his own class. Other versions say she was a high-born woman in love with a poor man, whom she dared not marry.

Her mind snapped one night and she drowned her children—a boy and a girl, maybe 6 and 8 years old. She walks the hills and the gulches in the nights, weeping and looking for her children. Until she finds them—or steals yours—she is doomed to walk and weep and search.

To hear nostalgic residents of long-gone mining camps tell it, there must be other, happier ghosts out there in the jagged hills. Smiling about the wealth wrested from the reluctant, dangerous rock. Happy about the rich, colorful life of the mining camps, where all kinds of people earned a special camaraderie.

Let us dispose first of Arizona's best-known mine, the Lost Dutchman, which may have been entirely a phantom. Reclusive, German-born prospector Jacob Walz was bringing gold out of the

Superstition Mountains east of Phoenix in the 1870s and 1880s. It supposedly was from an old Spanish mine in those mountains, not the best suited geologically to hold massive amounts of gold.

Walz died in 1891 without disclosing the whereabouts of his mine. Since then, many prospectors have invested their fortunes, and sometimes their lives, in the search for a mine that may or may not have been located in the brooding Superstitions. They're still at it, and the mysteries and legends seem stronger with every passing season.

It was proven, palpable gold and silver deposits that brought the first U.S. prospectors to Arizona Territory. In the 1850s they worked old Spanish and Mexican mines in southern Arizona, and developed a few new sites. In 1862, La Paz on the Colorado River became a short-lived boom town.

Soon after, mountain man Pauline Weaver led a party of easterners to Rich Hill at the south end of the Bradshaw Mountains. Jonathan Richmond, a court clerk in the first territorial governing party sent west, wrote home to his parents in Ohio: "Here is where gold was found on the top of a mountain and from forty to fifty thousand dollars taken out with jack-knives. What do you think of such diggings? There is no gold to be found about there except on the very summit of the mountain, which is in the hands of a few men."

Richmond also reported on the high price of groceries, when they could be purchased at all: "Provisions are at present very high, flour .25 cents [a pound], bacon .60 cents, coffee $1.00, sugar $1.00, eggs $1.00, doz, the rest in proportion."

Other gold and silver mining districts were more enduring than Rich Hill. A few miles north, and a few months later, the Walker Party discovered the bonanza that would support the town of Prescott. Some mines, like the Silver King southeast of Phoenix, created huge fortunes for their owners. Silver King principal William Boyce Thompson endowed Boyce Thompson Southwest Arboretum, a unique desert botanical garden that is now an Arizona state park.

While some of the gold and silver properties lasted well into this

century, there was a massive shift to copper before 1900. These were labor-intensive mines, deep shafts at first, then vast open pits.

Substantial cities developed around these mines: Clifton and later Morenci on the eastern Arizona border. Bisbee and the smelter town of Douglas in the southeast. Jerome on Cleopatra Hill above the Verde Valley, and a semi-circle of satellite towns below. Globe, a former silver mining town east of Phoenix, and the newer towns of Miami, Inspiration, Claypool. Superior was another, named not out of intense civic pride, but for a mining company.

Workers from many nations flocked to these new camps: Irishmen, Bohemians, Czechs, Moravians, Serbians, Italians, Armenians, Germans. Mexicans were recruited periodically, depending on labor demand and U.S. feelings about their country; eventually, families of Mexican descent made up much of the population of Arizona's mining towns.

The people shared their cultures, and yet each culture remained intact. While there were often racial tensions, one old-timer recalls, "We looked out for each other. We were kind of like a family."

At a fire department picnic or a church potluck supper, the piquant entrees of Eastern Europe blended with the spicy foods of Mexico. Desserts might include Slavic scrolls and Mexican *empanadas*.

Copper mines are rarely in convenient locations. Towns like Jerome, Bisbee and Clifton were built on steep mountain faces or in twisting canyons. Business buildings were shaped to fit, and homes, sometimes on stilts, were tucked into every nook and pocket.

Clifton's first jail was blasted and chiseled out of solid rock in a canyon wall. Its first prisoner was the man who built it, jailed after a drunken toot to celebrate its completion. Jerome's jail slid 300 feet downhill in 1925, taking the post office with it.

The highway through Jerome crosses a hogback with homes clinging to either side of the road, and an abyss beyond. A 1930s-era newspaperman decided "The Hogback" lacked glamour and so he

Desert Botanical Garden, Phoenix

renamed it: Swine Crest.

Danger increased the camaraderie of the people in the mining camps. Deaths and injuries were frequent. When an accident took out a miner, his friends passed a lunch bucket at the mine gate to collect money for his family. Each town was devastated by at least one major fire, as were most frontier communities. Clifton and Bisbee suffered heavy floods through their canyons.

The big mines attracted their own railroads, and Bisbee even had a streetcar line. Jerome and Bisbee were major southwestern cities early in this century, and they drew traveling theater troupes of all sorts. Later, movie houses were built in all of the camps. Band concerts were frequent. Each town had a good range of churches, civic and fraternal organizations.

Holidays were occasions for community blowouts. A big one was Cinco de Mayo (May 5), a Mexican national holiday. And the Fourth of July was always good for a major celebration, perhaps the biggest of the year. Then the proud, competitive volunteer fire companies showed off their skills. Hose companies raced to see who could roll out their cart, hook a hose to a hydrant and get water through it. And the miners competed in drilling contests, using the simple tools used to punch holes in rock before power tools came along. A single-jack team was one man holding a shaft of drill steel while another hammered it with a sledge hammer; a double-jack team was one very brave man holding while two men hammered alternately.

The holes thus drilled were packed with explosives which loosened the rock faces. Even in the 1970s, long after drilling had become highly mechanized, Bisbee used to brace itself daily for the 3 p.m. blast in the Lavendar Pit mine at the foot of Tombstone Canyon.

The towns had proud high schools of course, and their athletes tended to be big and rough. Football fields were built atop waste dumps or slag heaps, meaning a loose ball which went over the edge usually ended up 300 feet below.

The football players said their cheerleaders—indeed, all the women in town—had pretty legs, formed by walking up and down hills. Visitors from the flatlands tended to agree.

Mines were subject to the whims of world copper prices. Labor strife was frequent. But what finally determines the future of such a town is the size and sometimes the location of its ore body.

In the 1950s, it was found that Ray and Sonora were in the way of Kennecott's big pit southeast of Phoenix. Thousands of Arizonans found their hometowns vanishing, to be replaced by the new town called Kearny. Similarly, mines in the Clifton area ate Old Morenci (replaced by a new town) and Metcalfe (which simply disappeared).

Jerome's last mines shut down in the 1950s, and the town was on the ropes for a while. Then civic boosters got busy turning it into one of the West's best-known "ghost towns." Jerome had a special advantage: Its mountain perch offers a breath-taking view of the Verde Valley and the Red Rocks area around Sedona. Around Halloween, visitors and former residents gather for Spook Night, a reunion, dance and barbecue. The mansion of James S. "Rawhide Jimmy" Douglas, who developed one of the area's richest mines, is now a state park.

Bisbee, still a lively place to live, is the scene of fanciful Halloween "bewitchment." People wear costumes and go partying up and down Tombstone Canyon and Brewery Gulch. "It feels natural, because you have to be a little weird to live here," one giddy resident explained.

Ajo, whose mine and smelter shut down in 1985, had a little harder time of it. But now it is coming back as a modest tourist town and a place to retire on the healthy desert of southwestern Arizona. It's not far from Organ Pipe Cactus National Monument and the popular border crossing into Mexico at Lukeville.

Ajo's name means "garlic" in Spanish, and newcomers want to pronounce it with a long "a" instead of the Spanish "AH-hoe." Locals tell about the European tourists who stopped for refreshments at the Dairy Queen ice cream store.

"We do not know how to say the name of this place," one tourist said to a waitress. "Would you pronounce it for us?"

Very politely, the waitress sounded it out: "DARE-ee Queen."

The mining districts around Globe-Miami and Clifton-Morenci are still in business, although market conditions and labor strife in the early 1980s caused a major shakeout of the work force.

One of the healthier mining camps in Arizona is San Manuel, northeast of Tucson, developed in 1954. Someone not accustomed to Spanish pronunciation may hear the name as "Salmon Wells," a rather repelling notion.

The San Manuel mine is underground, and ore is taken out by "drift-caving," cutting tunnels and letting the interior of the mountain cave into them. Waiting railroad cars haul the ore away. It's not as dangerous as it sounds, given high-tech safeguards, and the temperature 2,600 feet underground is a constant eighty degrees, nice during the 100 degree plus Arizona summers.

Still, accidents do happen. Some years back, a young mining engineer was crushed by a rock. Miners wear loose rubber boots over their shoes, and the young engineer's boots were white.

Now White Boots prowls the drifts of the San Manuel mine, where most of the illumination comes from miners' headlamps. A miner intent on his job will look up into the darkness for a moment and see a pair of white boots walking, slowly walking.

MAIN DISHES

A standoff at La Fiesta De los Vaqueros Rodeo

Pickle Filled Franks

½ cup finely chopped Swiss cheese
⅓ cup cubed Arnold's Dill Pickles
1 tbsp prepared mustard
6 Schreiner's Fine Sausage
Frankfurters, Knockwurst or Weiners
6 slices Schreiner's Fine Sausage Bacon
6 Holsum Hot Dog Buns, split, toasted
and buttered

- Combine cheese, pickle and mustard; mix well.
- Split sausages in half, lengthwise, without cutting all the way through.
- Fill sausages with pickle mixture.
- Wrap bacon slice around each sausage.
- Arrange in shallow baking dish; bake in 350 degree oven 25 minutes, or until bacon is crisp.
- Serve in hot dog buns.
- Serves 6.

Monte Cristo Sandwiches

3 Laid in Arizona Eggs, beaten
⅓ cup milk
½ cup butter, softened
2 tsp prepared mustard
12 slices Holsum White Bread
6 slices Swiss cheese, cut in half
6 slices Beck's Smoked Cooked Ham
powdered sugar
cherry preserves

- Preheat oven to 425 degrees.
- Beat together eggs and milk; set aside.
- Beat together butter and mustard until well blended; spread on 1 side of each bread slice.
- For each sandwich, top 1 slice of bread with 1 slice of cheese, 1 slice of ham, a second slice of cheese and a second slice of bread, butter side down.
- Dip each sandwich in egg mixture; brown on both sides on lightly buttered griddle.
- Place on cookie sheet; bake 8-10 minutes.
- To serve, slice each sandwich in half diagonally; sprinkle with sugar and top with spoonful of preserves.
- Serves 6.

Black Bean Boboli

1 (12 oz) pkg Territorial Gourmet
Mexican Black Bean Soup/Salad Mix

2 small Boboli shells

1 cup grated UDA Seal of Arizona
Monterey Jack Cheese

1 (9 oz) jar Territorial Gourmet Salsa
De Las Catalinas-Verde

1 cup diced ripe Pavo Roma Tomatoes

2 cups shredded lettuce

sour cream for topping

cilantro or green onion to garnish

- Cook black beans according to pkg directions; drain and very lightly mash with fork.
- Spread beans on shell; top with cheese, salsa and tomato.
- Place in microwave oven 2 minutes, or until cheese melts.
- Top with lettuce.
- Garnish with sour cream and cilantro or onion.
- Serves 2-4.

Salsa Caliente Omelet

6 Laid In Arizona Eggs, at
room temperature

6 tbsp milk

dash pepper

½ tsp salt

2 tbsp UDA Seal of Arizona Butter

½ cup grated UDA Seal of Arizona
Longhorn Cheddar Cheese

4 slices Beck's Bacon, cooked
and chopped

1 small onion, diced

Desert Kettle Salsa Caliente to taste

- Beat eggs until fluffy.
- Add milk and seasoning; mix well.
- In large skillet, melt butter over medium heat.
- Pour omelet mixture into pan; cook over medium-high heat, lifting edges of omelet to let uncooked egg run underneath.
- Cook 15 minutes, or until edges are set and golden.
- Before folding, sprinkle with cheese, bacon pieces and diced onion.
- Fold omelet, place on warm plate, top with salsa and serve.
- Serves 4.

Pistachio-Veggie Pizza

1, 10" Arizona Brand® Flour Tortilla

¼ cup broccoli flowerets

¼ cup cauliflower flowerets

1 medium mushroom, sliced

¼ cup water

¼ cup coarsely chopped The Arizona Pistachio Company Pistachios

1 tbsp chopped fresh oregano
or
½ tsp dried oregano

2 tbsp sun-dried, oil packed tomatoes, drained

¼ cup shredded mozzarella or ricotta cheese

• Pierce tortilla several times with fork. Place between 2 sheets of white paper towels.

• Cook in microwave on HIGH 1-1½ minutes, or until tortilla is barely crisp; set aside.

• Place 2 connected paper towels on counter.

• Place broccoli, cauliflower and sliced mushroom directly over perforation in center.

• Fold over both sides, then ends to enclose vegetables. Place on microwave plate, perforated side up.

• Pour water over towel to moisten.

• Cook on HIGH 2 minutes.

• Carefully pull open perforation; arrange vegetables on tortilla.

• Sprinkle top with pistachios, oregano, tomatoes and cheese.

• Return pizza to microwave; cook on HIGH 45-60 seconds, or just until cheese melts.

• Serve immediately.

• Serves 1.

Grand Canyon South Rim

Deep Dish Lamb-Sausage Pizza

2 lbs ground Arizona Lamb

2 tsp minced garlic

2 Fresh Touch Gardens Shallots, chopped

2 Fresh Touch Gardens Jalapeno Peppers, seeded and minced

4 tbsp fresh chopped cilantro

2 tsp salt

2 tsp Fresh Touch Gardens Oregano Leaves

1 tsp allspice

2 tbsp chili powder

4 tbsp apple cider vinegar

2 (1 lb) loaves frozen bread dough, thawed

4 tbsp olive oil

2 cups julienned red bell pepper

2 cups sliced Copperhead Leeks

2 cups prepared pizza sauce

4 tbsp sliced Arnold's Green Olives

3 cups shredded UDA Seal of Arizona Mozzarella Cheese

4 oz feta cheese, crumbled

- Combine first 10 ingredients in glass bowl. Cover and refrigerate overnight.
- Stretch or roll dough to fit 2, 12" greased pizza pans; set aside.
- In large skillet, cook lamb mixture until browned, about 5 minutes; drain well.
- Wipe skillet dry; add oil, sauté peppers; add leeks and cook until crisp tender.
- Spread ½ of pizza sauce over each crust.
- Layer lamb mixture, peppers and leeks, olives and cheeses equally on top.
- Bake in preheated 450 degree oven 10 minutes, until crust is golden brown.
- Serves 4-6.

Black Tie Pizza

1 (4 oz) jar Territorial Gourmet Olé Pasta Sauce

1 large Boboli shell

1 cup pitted black olives

1 cup thinly sliced red onion

6 oz crumbled feta cheese

1 (4 oz) jar Territorial Gourmet Olé Pesto Sauce

- Preheat oven to 400 degrees.
- Spread pasta sauce over pizza shell.
- Arrange olives and red onions on shell.
- Top with feta cheese; dot with pesto sauce.
- Bake 5-7 minutes, or until cheese is melting and sauce bubbling.
- Serves 4.

Cheese Souffle

grated Parmesan cheese

¼ cup UDA Seal of Arizona Butter

¼ cup all-purpose flour

¼ tsp salt

dash cayenne

1 cup milk

2 cups shredded UDA Seal of Arizona Cheddar Cheese

¼ cup grated Parmesan cheese

5 egg yolks, slightly beaten

5 egg whites

¼ tsp cream of tartar

- Preheat oven to 350 degrees.
- Butter 2 qt souffle dish or casserole.
- Sprinkle enough Parmesan cheese in souffle dish to coat bottom and sides evenly; remove any excess.
- Melt butter in saucepan; blend in flour, salt and cayenne.
- Remove from heat; stir in milk.
- Heat to boiling, stirring constantly. Boil and stir 1 minute.
- Remove from heat; stir in cheeses until melted.
- If necessary, return to low heat to finish melting cheeses. Do not boil.
- Blend a little hot mixture into egg yolks; return all to saucepan and blend thoroughly; set aside.
- Beat egg whites until frothy. Add cream of tartar; beat until soft peaks form.
- Fold cheese sauce into egg whites.
- Turn into souffle dish.
- Bake 40-45 minutes.
- Serves 6.

Variation:
- After folding in egg whites, fold in 1 (10 oz) pkg frozen, chopped broccoli which has been cooked and drained.

Cheese 'N' Vegetable Dinner

4 cups uncooked Ladson's
Medium Noodles

¼ cup UDA Seal of Arizona Butter

½ cup chopped onion

¼ cup all-purpose flour

¼ tsp dry mustard

2 cups milk

1¼ cups shredded UDA Seal of Arizona
Cheddar Cheese

¼ cup crumbled UDA Seal of Arizona
Blue Cheese

1 (10 oz) pkg frozen peas and carrots,
cooked and drained

4 hard boiled eggs, sliced

1-2 tbsp melted butter

1 slice Holsum Wheat Bread, cubed

- Preheat oven to 350 degrees.
- Cook noodles according to pkg directions; drain and set aside.
- Melt butter in 1½ qt saucepan; sauté onion until tender. Stir in flour and mustard.
- Remove from heat; gradually stir in milk.
- Heat to boiling, stirring constantly. Boil and stir 1 minute.
- Remove from heat; stir in cheeses.
- If necessary, return to low heat to finish melting cheeses. Do not boil.
- Place ½ of noodles in buttered 2 qt casserole; top with ½ of peas and carrots and ½ of egg slices.
- Pour ½ of cheese sauce over top. Repeat layers.
- Toss bread cubes in butter; place on top of casserole.
- Bake 30 minutes. Let stand 5 minutes before serving.
- Serves 6.

Eggs Salsa

12 Laid In Arizona Eggs

½ cup melted margarine

½ cup all-purpose flour

1 lb diced Cheddar cheese

1 (8 oz) ctn Carnation® Cottage Cheese

½ tsp salt

¼ tsp pepper

1 (4 oz) can diced green chilies

1 cup Miguel's Medium Salsa

- Mix all ingredients together.
- Place in greased casserole dish.
- Bake at 350 degrees ½ hour, or until done.
- Serve hot.
- Serves 8-10.

Grand Canyon grandeur

Onion Omelet, Italian Style

2 tsp UDA Seal of Arizona Butter,
divided

½ cup cooked, slivered Beck's Ham

½ cup thinly sliced onion

8 Laid in Arizona Eggs

½ cup milk

½ tsp salt

¾ cup shredded UDA Seal of Arizona
Cheddar Cheese

freshly ground black pepper

- Preheat oven to 350 degrees.
- Melt 1 tsp butter in small skillet; sauté ham and onion until onion is tender and ham is lightly browned; set aside.
- Mix eggs, milk and salt with fork.
- Melt remaining butter in 10″ omelet pan or heavy skillet until just hot enough to sizzle a drop of water.
- Pour in egg mixture (mixture should set along edges at once).
- With pancake turner, carefully draw cooked portions at edges toward center, so uncooked portions flow to bottom.
- Tilt skillet since it is necessary to hasten flow of uncooked eggs.
- Slide pan rapidly back and forth over heat to keep mixture in motion and sliding freely.
- While top is still moist and creamy looking, sprinkle with half of cheese, spoon on onion and ham; sprinkle with remaining cheese.
- Wrap handle of skillet with foil if it is not ovenproof.
- Bake 2-3 minutes, just until cheese melts.
- Serve with freshly ground pepper.
- Serves 4.

Egg and Chorizo Bake

½ lb chorizo
½ cup chopped onion
2 cloves garlic, chopped
diced green pepper
1 (5 oz) can diced green chilies
12 Hickman's Extra Large Eggs, beaten
1 tsp salt
½ cup shredded Cheddar cheese

- Brown chorizo in skillet with onion, garlic and green pepper.
- Add green chilies. Cook until chorizo is done.
- Pour eggs into skillet; stir, but do not let set. Add salt.
- Pour into large, buttered baking dish. Spread cheese evenly over mixture.
- Bake at 350 degrees 15 minutes, or until knife inserted in center comes out clean.
- Serves 6-8.

Pecan Quiche

1 cup cooked chicken, finely chopped
1 cup grated UDA Seal of Arizona Swiss Cheese
¼ cup chopped onion
1 tbsp all-purpose flour
½ cup chopped Country Estate Pecans
1, 9" baked pie shell
2 eggs, beaten
1 cup milk
½ tsp brown mustard

- Mix chicken, cheese, onion, flour and pecans.
- Sprinkle into cooled crust.
- Mix eggs, milk and mustard. Pour over chicken.
- Bake in 325 degree oven 50 minutes.
- Serves 6-8.

Asparagus Tomato Quiche

4 large Hickman's Eggs, beaten
3 tbsp all-purpose flour
1 tsp paprika
1 tsp salt
½ tsp dry mustard
1½ cups half and half
2½ cups grated UDA Seal of Arizona Swiss Cheese
1 pkg frozen whole asparagus spears
1, 10″ partially baked pie shell
1 large tomato, sliced into ¼″ slices

- Preheat oven to 375 degrees.
- Beat eggs with next 4 ingredients; add half and half and cheese.
- Reserving 6 asparagus spears for the top, chop remaining into 1″ lengths. Spread on bottom of pie shell; pour in liquid.
- Bake 25 minutes. Remove and quickly arrange tomato and asparagus on top in wagon wheel pattern.
- Bake additional 30 minutes or until knife inserted in center comes out clean.
- Serves 6-8.

Tostada De Carne

1 lb ground Arizona Beef
½ tsp salt
1 clove garlic, minced
¼ lb mushrooms, sliced
1 cup Desert Rose Red or Green Salsa
4 large flour tortillas
1 tbsp olive oil
2 cups chopped Copperhead Green Onions
2 cups chopped green bell peppers
1 (2 oz) can chopped black olives
2 cups grated Monterey Jack cheese
½ cup freshly grated Parmesan cheese
2 medium avocados, sliced
2 cups sour cream

- Brown beef in skillet sprinkled with salt.
- Drain drippings; add garlic, mushrooms and salsa.
- Cook over high heat until liquid evaporates.
- Brush tortillas with oil and place on pizza pans.
- Spread meat sauce on tortillas.
- Scatter green onion, bell pepper, olives and cheeses over top.
- Bake at 475 degrees until cheese is melted and bubbly, about 10 minutes.
- Arrange avocado slices on top.
- Cut into wedges and serve with sour cream.
- Serves 4.

Santa Cruz Tacos

1 lb ground beef
½ onion, chopped
½ cup Santa Cruz Chili Paste
2 tsp Santa Cruz Mexican Spice Mix
1 tsp salt
1 doz taco shells
grated UDA Seal of Arizona Longhorn Cheese
shredded lettuce
chopped tomatoes
Santa Cruz Picante Sauce

- Brown ground beef in large skillet.
- Stir in onions and sauté until tender.
- Add chili paste, salt and spice mix; stir to mix.
- Cover skillet; cook over low heat 10-15 minutes.
- Fill taco shells with meat mixture.
- Garnish with grated cheese, shredded lettuce, chopped tomatoes and picante sauce.
- Serves 4-6.

Mama's Empanadas

2 cups cooked, shredded beef
1 (16 oz) can Rosarita® Spicy Refried Beans
½ cup Rosarita® Mild Chunky Picante Sauce
1 cup shredded Cheddar cheese
¼ tsp ground cumin
2 (1 lb) loaves frozen bread dough, thawed and each cut into eighths
1 egg, beaten

- In bowl, blend together first 5 ingredients; set aside.
- Flatten each bread dough section into 5″ circle.
- Spoon ¼ cup meat filling into center of each dough half.
- Fold dough over filling to make half circle. Press edges together with fork to seal.
- Place empanadas on lightly greased baking sheet; cover with plastic wrap and let rise in warm place 15-20 minutes.
- Remove wrap, brush with egg and bake at 350 degrees 20-25 minutes, or until golden brown.
- Makes 16 empanadas.

Pork Chip Chalupas

1 (3-4 lb) Beck's Boneless Pork Butt or
Pork Roast
4 cups water
1 (16 oz) bag pinto beans
3 cloves garlic, minced
2 bay leaves
1 tbsp salt
1 tbsp ground cumin
1 tbsp mild chili powder
1 jar Big Juan's Hot or Mild
Fresh Salsa
Territorial Gourmet Blue Corn Chips
sour cream

- Place pork in large slow cooker; add water.
- Place pinto beans around roast; add next 5 ingredients.
- Cook on high 4-5 hours, adding salsa the last 30 minutes of cooking.
- Serve over corn chips and top with sour cream.
- Serves 4-6.

Mad Coyote Cheese Enchiladas

12 Arizona Brand® Corn Tortillas
½ cup vegetable oil
1 lb Monterey Jack cheese, grated
1 lb mild Cheddar cheese, grated
1 large onion, finely diced
sour cream, chopped green onions,
olives, green chilies, guacamole
to garnish

Enchilada Sauce:
3½ cups chicken broth
1 yellow onion, diced
1 tbsp cooking oil
1 pkg Mad Coyote Enchilada Mix
⅛ cup all-purpose flour
⅛ cup cold water

- For enchilada sauce, mix together broth, onion, oil and enchilada mix.
- Let boil 10 minutes.
- Mix flour and water into a smooth paste; slowly add paste to mixture.
- Simmer, uncovered, 1½ hours, stirring occasionally.
- Meanwhile, heat skillet, fry corn tortillas in oil to soften.
- Pour small amount of enchilada sauce in baking dish to coat bottom.
- Mix cheeses together; fill each tortilla with cheese and onion.
- Roll the filled tortillas; place seam side down in baking dish.
- Top with remaining cheese, onions and sauce.
- Bake at 350 degrees 18-20 minutes.
- Garnish with sour cream, chopped green onions, olives, green chilies and guacamole.
- Serves 6.

Spinach Enchiladas

Enchilada Sauce:
½ cup chopped onion

2 cloves garlic, peeled and crushed

2 tbsp UDA Seal of Arizona Butter

1 (28 oz) can Italian plum tomatoes

1 (6 oz) can tomato paste

2 canned green chilies

1 tsp salt

1 tsp sugar

1 tsp crushed cumin

Spinach Filling:
1 lb fresh Copperhead Spinach

½ cup water

1/ tsp instant chicken bouillon

½ tsp salt

1 cup sour cream

Enchiladas:
12, 6" soft flour tortillas

butter

1½ cups shredded UDA Seal of Arizona Monterey Jack cheese

sweet peppers to garnish

- For sauce, sauté onion and garlic in butter.
- Place in blender with tomatoes, tomato paste, chilies, salt, sugar and cumin; blend.
- Pour into saucepan and simmer, uncovered, 15 minutes. Keep warm.
- For filling, cook spinach in water with chicken bouillon and salt until barely tender. Drain well; chop. Combine with sour cream.
- Preheat oven to 350 degrees.
- To assemble enchiladas, lightly brown each tortilla over medium heat on both sides in lightly buttered skillet until heated thoroughly and softened but not crisp.
- Dip each warm tortilla in enchilada sauce. Spoon 3 tbsp filling over each tortilla and roll up.
- Spoon a little of the enchilada sauce into buttered 13" x 9" x 2" baking dish.
- Arrange filled enchiladas, seam down; cover with remaining sauce.
- Cover tightly with foil and bake 20-25 minutes.
- Remove foil; sprinkle on cheese. Return to oven 3-5 minutes to melt cheese.
- Garnish with sweet peppers, if desired.
- Serves 6.

Authentic Southwestern Enchiladas

2 lbs Arizona Beef Brisket or Chuck,
cut in cubes

2 cups water, lightly salted

½ cup Santa Cruz Chili Powder

3 tbsp Santa Cruz Mexican Spice Mix

1 tbsp parsley

2 tbsp all-purpose flour

2 tbsp oil

24 Arizona Brand® Flour Tortillas

shredded lettuce, grated Cheddar or
Monterey Jack cheese to garnish

- Add meat to 2 cups salted water and cook ½ hour; save broth.
- While meat is stewing, mix in chili powder, spice mix and parsley.
- When meat is done, strain off broth.
- In large skillet, brown flour in oil; slowly stir in broth.
- Combine with meat and simmer 1½ hours, or until tender.
- Spoon some mixture on lower third of flour tortilla.
- Fold sides in; fold tortilla over mixture.
- Top with enchilada sauce, shredded lettuce and grated cheese, if desired.
- Serves 8-10.

Squash and Sausage Casserole

2 lbs yellow squash, sliced ½" thick

4 tbsp butter

2 medium onions, sliced

1 clove garlic, finely chopped

1 cup milk

1 cup Holsum Bread Crumbs

1 lb Beck's Sausage, cooked
and crumbled

4 eggs, lightly beaten

1½ cups grated sharp Cheddar cheese

1 cup chopped The Pecan Store Pecans

½ tsp salt

pepper

Topping:

4 tbsp melted butter

½ cup Holsum Bread Crumbs

½ cup chopped The Pecan Store Pecans

- Grease 2 qt casserole and set aside.
- Cook squash in heavy pan, adding enough water to cover.
- Bring to boil; reduce heat and simmer until squash is soft enough to mash. Drain and mash.
- Melt butter in separate pan, add onions and garlic; sauté until soft. Add squash.
- Heat milk and stir in bread crumbs, sausage, eggs, cheese, pecans, salt and pepper; pour into buttered casserole.
- For topping, combine melted butter, bread crumbs and pecans.
- Sprinkle over casserole.
- Bake in 350 degree oven 30 minutes.
- Serves 4-6.

Mexi-Pork Casserole

Filling:

1 lb ground pork

½ tsp salt

½ tsp Santa Cruz Chili Powder

1 cup shredded Cheddar cheese

½ cup Territorial Gourmet
Barbecue Sauce

1½ cans Mexicorn whole kernel
corn, drained

1 (8 oz) can tomato sauce

Crust:

1 cup Silver Creek Mill Whole
Wheat Flour

½ cup Silver Creek Mill Yellow
Corn Meal

2 tbsp sugar

1 tsp salt

1 tsp baking powder

¼ cup butter

½ cup milk

1 egg, beaten

1 cup shredded Cheddar cheese, divided

- Brown pork; stir in remaining filling ingredients and set aside.
- To prepare crust, stir together flour, corn meal, sugar, salt and baking powder; cut in butter.
- Blend in milk, egg and half the cheese.
- Spread crust mixture over bottom and sides of greased 9″ baking pan.
- Pour filling into crust; bake in 400 degree oven 25-30 minutes.
- Sprinkle with remaining cheese during last few minutes of baking.
- Serves 6-8.

Dilled Ham and Spinach Cheesecake

1⅓ cups whole grain rye cracker crumbs

¼ cup melted butter

1½ tsp Sahuaro Spice Co. Dillweed, divided

2 tbsp vegetable oil

½ cup minced onion

⅓ cup minced green bell pepper

1 (10 oz) pkg frozen chopped spinach, thawed and squeezed dry

1 (12 oz) ctn ricotta cheese

1 cup shredded Gouda cheese

4 Hickman's Eggs

¾ lb Goldmark Ham, diced

2 tbsp Arnold's Pickle Relish

1 cup Foremost® Sour Cream, divided

- Preheat oven to 300 degrees.
- Combine cracker crumbs and butter in small bowl.
- Press firmly onto bottom of 8″ springform pan. Sprinkle with ½ tsp dillweed; set aside.
- Heat oil in large skillet; sauté onion and green pepper until onion is tender.
- Add spinach; cook and stir 3 minutes; cool.
- Mix together cheeses in large bowl.
- Add eggs, 1 at a time, beating well after each addition.
- Stir in ham, spinach mixture, pickle relish, ⅓ cup sour cream and ½ tsp dillweed. Spread over crumbs.
- Bake 1 hour 20 minutes, or until center is set.
- Turn off oven; keep cheesecake in oven with door slightly open, 1 hour.
- Combine remaining sour cream and remaining dillweed. Spread on top of cheesecake.
- Serve immediately.
- Serves 6.

IF THEY COULD SEE HER NOW

"Tucson was as foreign a town [in 1869] as if it were in Hayti instead of within our own borders. The language, dress, funeral processions, religious ceremonies, feasts, dances, games, joys, perils, griefs and tribulations of its population were something not to be looked for in the region east of the Missouri River."
    —Army Captain John G. Bourke, *On The Border With Crook.*

For several decades after 1846, writing exaggerated descriptions of exotic Tucson was a favorite sport of Americans who passed through, or came to stay: soldiers, surveyors, California 49ers, stagecoach passengers, journalists.

Yet the *Yanquis* were drawn to Arizona's largest city in increasing numbers. On a rainy March day in 1856, a handful of frontiersmen pieced together a flag pole from pieces of mesquite wood. They prepared to raise the U.S. flag from the roof of a tiny store in the plaza at Tucson.

The area had belonged to the United States for nearly two years, but U.S. soldiers had yet to occupy Tucson. Mexican residents were packing up and trekking south, escorted by a ragged band of Mexican soldiers.

The acting Mexican commandant, whose father had been an earlier commander of the presidio of Tucson, asked the *Norteamericanos* to delay their flag-raising. They ignored him, and soon the Mexicans exited the town, plodding sadly southward in the rain.

None of the participants could have dreamed what Tucson would become during the next 130 years: a bright, bustling, sprawling city of nearly half a million people, rich in layered cultures.

The 1848 Treaty of Guadalupe Hidalgo established the U.S.-Mexico boundary at the Gila River, sixty miles north of Tucson. But the United States coveted the mineral wealth reputed to be south of the Gila. More importantly, powerful southerners in Congress wanted to secure a southern railroad route to the Pacific, in case slavery divided the nation.

President Franklin Pierce sent South Carolina railroad president and diplomat James Gadsden to deal with Mexican President Antonio Lopez de Santa Anna. For ten million dollars, Santa Anna sold the southern portions of what would become Arizona and New Mexico. Congress approved the deal in the summer of 1854.

You could fill a moderate-sized book with the witty, nasty writings of early gringos about Tucson. J. Ross Browne, writing for *Harper's New Magazine* after a trip west in 1864, wrote of "a city of mud-boxes, dingy and dilapidated, cracked and baked into a composite of dust and filth; littered about with broken corrals, sheds, bake-ovens, carcasses of dead animals, and broken pottery; barren of verdure, parched, naked, and grimly desolate in the glare of a southern sun. Adobe walls without whitewash inside or out, hard earth floors, baked and dried Mexicans, sore-backed burros, coyote dogs, and terra-cotta children . . ."

Browne's description of the Americans who congregated there was no more flattering. Yet the individualistic early settlers built an enduring city. Some of the former Mexican settlers returned, and other Mexicans followed.

C.L. Sonnichsen's splendidly readable history of Tucson quotes Hilario Gallengo, who was born in Tucson in 1850: "When we needed provisions we made a lot of rag dolls and took them over to the Gila River where there were Pima and Maricopa Indian settlements and traded them for tepary beans, corn, wheat and black-eyed peas. From around home we gathered mesquite beans and dried them and ground them into pinole [a kind of flour]."

Captain Bourke wrote of the menu in 1869 at a Tucson boarding house he called the Shoo-Fly: "Beef was not always easy to procure, but there was no lack of bacon, chicken, mutton and kid meat. Potatoes ranked as luxuries of the first class . . . and often could not be had for love or money.

"There was plenty of 'jerked' [dried] beef, savory and palatable enough in stew and hashes; eggs and the sweet, toothsome black 'frijoles' [pinto beans] of Mexico."

Fresh vegetables were grown locally, but fresh fruit came sporadically on burro pack trains from Mexico, depending on the mood of Apache raiders. Here and elsewhere in his writings about Arizona, Bourke described reliance in hard times on dried, black Mexican figs.

Even as Tucson grew into a modern American city, its ties with Mexico gave it a distinctively Hispanic flavor in architecture and outlook. Its *barrios*, Hispanic neighborhoods which tend to be anonymous in other southwestern cities, are intact and identifiable in Tucson. In Tucson's downtown district, it has preserved many adobe dwellings that date from territorial days.

The town is ringed by rugged mountains, most notably the Santa Catalina range on its north side. Saguaro National Monument, celebrating the towering cactus that symbolizes the Southwest, is divided into two sections, east and west of the city.

Tucsonans were upset when the legislature foisted the University of Arizona on them in 1885. What kind of patronage jobs could a university provide? They would rather have had the insane asylum, plucked off by upstart and ambitious Phoenix. But the university has since become a magnet for culture and for science, allowing Tucson to think of itself as the Athens of Arizona.

Here is a bit of irony, and that is an intentional, double pun: Hispanic blacksmiths and armorers of Tucson Presidio, lacking most normal amenities, used for their anvils the iron of meteorite fragments, hauled laboriously from nearby mountains. Today Tucson is something of a world capital for astronomy, having more telescopes within fifty miles than any other city. The meteorite fragments, by the way, are in the Smithsonian Institution.

Tucson is headquarters for the Western Music Association of America, celebrating the old cowboy songs. The Sons of the Pioneers winter in Tucson. Arizona-born Rex Allen lives on a ranch nearby, and drives to a Tucson studio to record the voice-over narrations that have done as much as his music to make him a household baritone. A better-known singer, perhaps, is Linda Ronstadt, who in recent years has been promoting and singing Mariachi music. Her Mexican grandfather, Federico Ronstadt, was a pioneer wagon-maker and hardware dealer in Tucson.

There's a contrast in pop culture west of Tucson, through a gap in the Tucson Mountains. Here is Old Tucson, an old-west amusement park used occasionally as a movie set, and the nearby Arizona-Sonora Desert Museum, a sensitive exhibition of the plants and wildlife of the region.

Tucson clearly is the hub of James Gadsden's purchase, but the cradle of European civilization in Arizona was at Tubac, forty-two miles south. Tubac was never more than a village, although today it is an upscale village, occupied by those who can afford to live where they want.

Its homes, boutiques and galleries, of burnt adobe and slump block, are tucked between Interstate 19 and the bed of the Santa Cruz River. Across the river, and northeast of the town, Mt. Wrightson rises to 9,453 feet.

The highway leads to the border of Mexico at Nogales, an upstart town built in the 1880s, when railroads crossed the border. Tourists looking for a taste of Mexico are likely to overlook Tubac's modest signs.

At Tubac State Historic Park, dioramas show how the old Spanish presidio, first established in 1752, commanded the valley of the Santa Cruz. A taped narration by Will Rogers Jr., a long-time Tubac resident, explains the town's history. Rogers' Spanish pronunciation is awful, but he clearly explains why Tubac was so important in Arizona history.

Apache raids, and a lack of support from the government in Mexico City, forced Hispanic settlers to abandon Tubac more than once. It was derelict, in fact, when American prospectors and investors occupied it in the 1850s and made it a center of mining activity.

Its early residents included Charles D. Poston, who later fancied himself "Father of Arizona," and his partner, Major Samuel P. Heintzelman, who had commanded Fort Yuma. Heintzelman would command the Union defense of Washington, D.C., during the Civil War, and use his presence in Washington to lobby for Arizona.

Heintzelman's diaries are a delight, frequently concerning themselves with the weather or the problems of obtaining food. The entry for September 16, 1858, included this commentary: "This afternoon I went and took a bath in the famous Santa Cruz River. When the water runs a mule could drink it dry, but I found a hole with water a little over knee-deep and that but a little over my length. There is however an Acequia (irrigation ditch) that draws off considerable. A few miles above or below there is no water running."

The museum also houses the press that printed Arizona's first newspaper, *The Weekly Arizonian*, for a few months in 1859. The editor, E.M. Cross, fought Arizona's first recorded duel with mining man Sylvester Mowry. Neither man won; after Cross expended his bullets, Mowry fired into the air, and they retired to tap a keg of whiskey.

The duelists were arguing over the matter of separating Arizona from New Mexico Territory. Cross opposed it; Mowry, Heintzelman and Poston all worked diligently to make Arizona a separate territory (and succeeded in 1863).

Mowry, another former officer from Fort Yuma, owned the Patagonia Mine southeast of Tubac. Mexicans first worked the mine, and several frontier U.S. military commanders owned shares in it before U.S. arms maker Samuel Colt acquired it in a hostile takeover late in the 1850s.

The mine lent its name to a district that is a special favorite among

Arizona's geographic insiders and knowing visitors from around the world. Its rolling grassy hills are not like much else in Arizona; the grassland scenes from the 1955 movie *Oklahoma!* were filmed here.

The hamlet of Patagonia occupies a shallow canyon along Sonoita Creek. There hasn't been a train come through since 1962, so the former freight yards are a city park and the picturesque old frame depot a city-county building.

The Nature Conservancy's bird sanctuary along the creek draws birders from around the world, and there's Anne Stradling's odd little Museum of the Horse.

My wife and I were dining in Patagonia not long ago when a family of Californians quizzed the waiter about Patagonia's attractions.

"That's all there is here?" the man of the family asked incredulously. "The Museum of the Horse and a Bird Sanctuary?"

A woman in Tucson, perhaps a native, had circled Patagonia in their tourist guide. To many Arizonans, the attraction of Patagonia is that it is not much spoiled by attractions.

Visitors sometimes encounter Robert Lenon, one of Patagonia's most loyal residents. He was a young college student when he first worked at the mines in the area in the 1920s. He couldn't move back until 1946. "But it was on my mind all the time," Lenon said. He had become a mining engineer, and for forty years ran his practice from a false-fronted building in Patagonia. He became an author and an expert on the history of the area. He can tell you about the nearby site of Fort Buchanan, the first U.S. army post established in the Gadsden Purchase, or the scattering of ghost towns in the hills southeast of Patagonia.

There do not seem to be two homes alike in Patagonia, a town of maybe 1,200 population. Some of the adobe homes on its back streets go back to Arizona's territorial days.

The woman from California was still fretting about the advisor in Tucson: "I don't know why she circled this place."

I could sympathize with her. Sometimes a traveler wants more excitement than Patagonia has to offer. Maybe I should have butted in and advised them to drive fifty miles east to Tombstone, which likes to call itself "The Town Too Tough To Die."

Prospector Ed Schieffelin in 1877 left the sanctuary of nearby Camp Huachua, against the advice of soldiers there. Apaches lurked in the hills. A military scout named Dan Leary warned Schieffelin he would find nothing but his tombstone.

When Schieffelin found a rich silver deposit, he called it the Tombstone claim, and the name stuck to the boom town that sprang up nearby. The picturesque name, and the legendary 1881 Gunfight at the O.K. Corral, has obscured some of the importance of Tombstone.

For a while in the 1880s, it was the largest, liveliest town between Texas and California. It had its share of outlaws and shootouts, but it also had lawmen, including Wyatt Earp and Bat Masterson. So most of the bad men congregated in the satellite towns of Charleston and Galeyville.

Touring theatrical companies from the U.S. and Mexico added Tombstone to their circuits, bringing everything from grand opera to trained dog acts. Until the mines began to fill with water in 1887, happy crowds filled the Bird Cage, the Crystal Palace, Schieffelin Hall.

These cultural elements may be missing from the town's reputation, but they are not forgotten. Entrepreneurs have restored many of Tombstone's historic buildings, including the theaters and saloons. There are museums and shops and a restored O.K. Corral. One of Tombstone's aptly-named newspapers, *The Epitaph*, today leads a double life. The local version is a community newspaper run by University of Arizona journalism students; the national edition is a lively journal of history.

The old Cochise County courthouse, built in 1882, is an Arizona State Historic Park. But the county seat was moved south in 1929 to the more enduring mining town of Bisbee, and that's another story from Mr. Gadsden's Purchase.

There's a narrow, winding canyon in the Mule Mountains called Tombstone Canyon, because it leads toward Tombstone. Here in 1877, some soldiers found ore and called their claim the Copper Queen, hoping it would rival another Arizona mine called the Silver King. In fact, the Copper Queen and other nearby mines surpassed the wealth of the Silver King many times over.

The town of Bisbee filled Tombstone Canyon, and spilled over into other boroughs. One of them is called Warren for George Warren, an alcoholic scout and prospector. Warren owned one-ninth of the Copper Queen. One day Warren was boasting that he could outrun a horse, and someone talked him into betting his mining claims on that boast. The horse was sober, and George was not, so he lost.

He died broke and sick, but his fame was assured in a couple of ways. In addition to having a place named for him, Warren's photograph was a model for the miner who appears on the Great Seal of the State of Arizona.

Bisbee made world news in July, 1917. Labor unions, including the troublesome Industrial Workers of the World (IWW, or "Wobblies") were trying to organize the mines. At the behest of the Phelps Dodge Corporation, Sheriff Harry Wheeler deputized "loyal" citizens of Bisbee. They rounded up 1,100 of their fellow citizens, marched them to a Phelps-Dodge-owned train, and shipped them out to Columbus, N.M.

The uproar over the "Bisbee Deportation" was enormous. A young attorney named Felix Frankfurter, later a liberal U.S. Supreme Court Justice, was sent to investigate. But nothing much ever came of the affair. The first of more than 200 citizens accused of kidnapping was acquitted, and charges against the others were dismissed.

The mines at Bisbee petered out in the 1970s, but the town is still a lively place to visit or live. Many retirees have moved in, along with some younger, free-thinking individualists and maybe a few social misfits.

The Bisbee Mining Museum does a good job of explaining the town's history in photograph and artifact. On an adjacent street, the Copper Queen Hotel still thrives as an old-fashioned hostelry and ex-officio museum. Bisbee insiders love to tell you about sin in Brewery Gulch, once the town's entertainment district.

Throughout the southeastern quarter of Arizona are isolated

mountain ranges that a writer a long time ago dubbed "sky islands." They are not connected to each other, although each is a segment of the Coronado National Forest.

Two of these islands, the Dragoon and Chiricahua mountains, were home to the Chiricahua Apaches, the people of Cochise and Geronimo, the last natives to resist subjugation by the white man.

Cochise died in 1874, and legend says he is buried at Cochise Stronghold in the Dragoons, now a pleasant picnic and hiking spot. He was succeeded by Geronimo, not a hereditary leader, but a strong one.

Most Apaches had capitulated by 1882, but for the following four years the Chiricahua raiders terrorized the region, flitting in and out of Mexico, usually operating in small bands. Soldiers from Fort Huachuca, usually operating deep in Mexico, doggedly pursued the Apaches.

An army travels on its stomach, especially when it is far from normal supply lines. Cornelius C. Smith Jr., who wrote a thorough history of Fort Huachuca, devoted quite a lot of space to the inadequacy of food on the frontier.

Smith quoted this request from Captain Henry W. Lawton, who led the final campaign against Geronimo, deep in the wilderness of northern Mexico: "I want not less than 500 rations of hard bread to be used on my foot marches when I attempt to move on an Indian camp. At that time, no animals can follow us and we must carry rations on our backs. We cannot have fires, so cannot bake flour."

Lawton's subsequent requests included bacon and flour for his base camps, and additional "field rations." Frequently, Lawton received fewer supplies than he asked for. Finally, in September, 1886, Geronimo was persuaded to come to Skeleton Canyon in the extreme southeastern corner of Arizona and surrender to the U.S. Army. A bloody era of western history was over.

Fort Huachuca is today a modern Army post. You can buy vittles anywhere in the Gadsden Purchase, from the supermarkets and five-star restaurants of Tucson to the cafe at Portal, on the east side of the Chiricahuas.

Bird watchers, campers and hikers pass through Portal to reach Cave Creek Canyon, one of several gorgeous canyons that drain the Chiricahua range. The American Museum of Natural History has a field station here to study the flora and fauna of the Chiricahuas.

On the other side of the mountains is Chiricahua National Monument, which includes an area of fantastic stone shapes called the Wonderland of Rocks.

There's still a lot of wildness here, and it's interesting to note how Captain Bourke remembered southeastern Arizona from 1869: "There were stretches of country picturesque to look upon and capable of farming, especially with irrigation; and other expanses not a bit more fertile than so many brick-yards, where all was desolation, the home of the cactus and the coyote. Arizona was in those days separated from 'God's Country' by more than fifteen hundred miles . . ."

There are some people in the Gadsden Purchase today who will tell you that the creator must have moved, joining the migration to the Southwest.

MEATS & FISH

Oak Creek Canyon, Sedona

Smokin' Hot Meatloaf

1 lb ground beef
¼ lb ground pork
¼ lb ground veal
1 large Pavo Bell Pepper, minced
1 large Copperhead Onion, minced
2 tsp Arizona Gunslinger Smokin' Hot Jalapeno Pepper Sauce
1 tsp salt
1 (8 oz) can tomato sauce
1 can water
2 cups cracker crumbs
3 eggs, well beaten
1 tsp Sahauro Spice Co. Celery Salt

- Combine all ingredients; bake at 350 degrees until vegetables are tender and flavors are well blended, about 1 hour.
- Serves 6-8.

La La La Bambas

1½-2 lbs Arizona Ground Beef
¼ tsp Sahuaro Spice Co. Ginger
2-3 medium large bananas, cut in large chunks
1 cup all-purpose flour
1 egg, beaten with 2 tsp water
2 cups shredded coconut
½ cup vegetable oil
2 cups beef broth
1 cup Desert Kettle Apricot Chutney
2 cups Dutch applesauce with cinnamon

- In mixing bowl, mix beef and ginger.
- Shape ground beef around banana chunks; roll in flour.
- Dip in egg mixture; roll in coconut.
- Cover; chill ½ hour.
- In large skillet, add oil; lightly brown meat chunks.
- Remove and drain meat chunks; discard oil.
- In skillet, pour in beef broth mixed with chutney. Add meat chunks; simmer 15 minutes.
- Add applesauce, cook 5 minutes.
- Serve with sauce from skillet.
- Serves 4.

Meat Balls Piemonte

2 lbs Goldmark Extra Lean
Ground Beef

½ clove garlic, crushed

1 medium onion, finely chopped

¼ tsp savory

¼ tsp oregano

¼ tsp paprika

2 tsp salt

1 cup Holsum Bread Crumbs

1 tbsp Sallie's Tarragon Mustard

dash hot pepper sauce

2 tsp Worcestershire sauce

all-purpose flour

4 strips Bar-S Bacon, cut into
small pieces

1 cup strong Espressions Coffee

½ cup Arizona Vineyards Blanc
White Burgundy

¾ cup water, divided

1 tsp salt

1 tsp sugar

1½ tbsp all-purpose flour

1 cup sour cream

- Combine meat, garlic, onion, herbs, salt, crumbs, mustard, hot pepper sauce and Worcestershire sauce; mix well.
- Form into 2½ doz balls. Dust with flour.
- Cook bacon until crisp and brown; remove from pan.
- Sauté meat balls in bacon drippings until lightly browned.
- Add coffee, wine, ½ cup water, salt and sugar. Simmer 15 minutes. Return bacon to pan.
- Stir in 1½ tbsp flour, mixed smooth with ¼ cup cold water.
- Cook gently 5 minutes longer. Reduce heat.
- Garnish with dollops of sour cream.
- Serves 6-8.

Grilled London Broil

1 btl low sodium soy sauce
1 tbsp diced fresh ginger
1 jalapeno, diced
1 (4-6 lb) London broil
Mad Coyote BBQ Dust
1 bag mesquite charcoal briquettes

- Mix soy sauce, ginger and jalapeno together.
- Marinate meat overnight in mixture.
- Dust heavily with barbecue seasoning.
- Cook over mesquite coals 2½-3 hours, or until desired doneness.
- Serves 8-10.

Territorial Days Pot Roast

4 lbs beef bottom round or rump roast
1 tsp ground ginger
2 tbsp Worcestershire sauce
1 cup R. W. Webb Arizona Sauvignon Blanc
2 tbsp chopped parsley
½ tsp freshly ground black pepper
2 medium onions, thinly sliced
1 cup Foremost® Sour Cream
2 tbsp grated horseradish

- In large pot or Dutch oven, brown meat on all sides. Do not add oil or fat.
- Add ginger, Worcestershire sauce, wine, parsley, pepper and onions. Cover pot; simmer on top of stove 2½-3 hours, or until tender.
- Combine sour cream with the horseradish.
- Thick slice meat, cover with gravy and top with dollop of sour cream mixture.
- Serves 6.

Steak Tino

10 cloves garlic, quartered
1 (4 lb) thick sirloin
4 tbsp pepper
½ (750 ml) btl Arizona Vineyards Sauterne
5 tbsp loose leaf basil
2 tbsp stone ground mustard
½ cup olive oil
3 tbsp salt

- Insert clove quarters in sirloin.
- Mix together next 6 ingredients.
- Place sirloin in pan and pour on marinade; marinate 1-2 hours.
- Remove, grill 15 minutes each side, basting frequently with marinade.
- Do not overcook. The meat will have a rare appearance due to the absorbed marinade.
- To serve, crosscut on grain.
- Serves 6-8.

Pistachio Stuffed Beef Filet

1 (3½-4 lb) beef filet, trimmed of fat

⅓ cup minced Fresh Touch
Gardens Shallots

1½ tsp minced Fresh Touch
Gardens Garlic

¼ cup Shamrock® Butter

½ lb button mushrooms

½ lb Shiitake mushrooms

1 cup R. W. Webb Arizona
Fume Blanc

¼ cup chopped Fresh Touch
Gardens Parsley

½ tsp salt

2 tbsp plus ½ tsp freshly ground black
pepper, divided

¼ cup brandy

4 cups Triple A Pistachios, lightly
roasted and coarsely chopped

2 tbsp Worcestershire sauce

butter

- Make pocket in filet.
- Sauté shallots and garlic in butter; add mushrooms, reducing any developing liquid.
- Add wine, stir in parsley, salt, ½ tsp pepper and brandy; simmer over low heat until liquid is reduced to 2 tbsp. Cool slightly.
- Add pistachios; fill filet cavity with mixture. Tie filet with cotton kitchen twine.
- Coat with Worcestershire sauce and 2 tbsp pepper.
- Sear filet in small amount of butter; bake in 425 degree oven to desired doneness.
- Slice into ¼" slices; serve with reduced stock sauce.
- Serves 8-10.

Tenderloin Neapolitan

3 lbs center cut beef tenderloin

½ cup pitted, sliced ripe olives

12 Pavo Cherry Tomatoes, cut in half

½ tsp dried basil

½ cup freshly grated Parmesan cheese

fresh parsley and whole Pavo Cherry
Tomatoes to garnish

Marinade:

¾ tsp salt

¼ tsp freshly ground black pepper

½ tsp Arizona Gunslinger Smokin' Hot
Jalapeno Pepper Sauce

½ tsp Arizona Champagne
Mustard Sauce

½ cup extra virgin olive oil

2 cloves garlic, minced

2 tbsp tarragon vinegar

2 tbsp fresh lemon juice

1 (8 oz) can sliced mushrooms, drained

- Whisk all marinade ingredients, except mushrooms, until well blended. Add mushrooms; toss.

- Trim membrane from tenderloin. Marinade beef in refrigerator 4-6 hours, turning occasionally.

- Preheat oven to 450 degrees.

- Remove beef from marinade; scrape off mushrooms and reserve for later use. Tie snugly with cotton string at 2″ intervals. Meat thermometer can be inserted into thickest part of roast. Place on rack in broiler pan.

- Bake 35 minutes, or until thermometer registers 135 degrees for medium.

- When cooked to desired doneness, set aside for 10 minutes to allow juices to settle.

- While roast is standing, drain mushrooms from marinade. Sauté mushrooms and black olives 5 minutes.

- Lower heat to simmer; add tomatoes and basil; cook 5 minutes.

- Set oven to broil. Remove string from roast; cut 8 slices 1″-1½″ thick.

- Arrange slices on ovenproof serving dish; top with mushrooms, olive and tomato mixture.

- Sprinkle with cheese; broil until cheese melts and is light brown.

- Remove from oven. Garnish with parsley and whole cherry tomatoes, if desired.

- Serves 8.

Coyote Fried Steak

1½ lbs Arizona Beef Round Steak
1¾ cups Carnation® Milk, divided
¾ cup mayonnaise
1 cup bread crumbs
1 cup grated Parmesan cheese
6 tbsp chili powder
½ tbsp cayenne
2 tbsp Sallie's Saltmix
½ tbsp cumin
1 tbsp salt
1 tbsp black pepper
vegetable oil
2 tbsp all-purpose flour
salt and pepper
1 tbsp tequila (optional)
orange wedges or lemon slices to garnish

- Cut round steak in 4-5 servings. Beat steak until tender and ½" thick.
- Mix ¼ cup milk and mayonnaise together. Mix bread crumbs, cheese, chili powder, cayenne, seasoning salt, cumin, salt and black pepper.
- Dip steaks in mayonnaise/milk mixture, then coat with bread crumb mixture.
- Heat about ¼" oil in skillet. Cook steak, 2 servings at a time, until brown on both sides.
- Remove from skillet; pour off oil, leaving about 3 tbsp in pan.
- Add flour, cooking over medium heat for 1-2 minutes. Add 1½ cups milk; stir until thickened.
- Add salt and pepper to taste.
- Stir in tequila, if desired.
- Serve sauce with steaks.
- Garnish with orange wedges or lemon slices.
- Serves 4-5.

Chorizo Sausage

½ cup Sahuaro Spice Co. Chorizo Mix
1 tbsp vinegar
½ cup water
1¾ lbs ground meat

- Mix ingredients together well.
- Shape as desired; fry to desired doneness.
- Serves 4-6.

Traditional Pork Loin Roast

3½-4 lb Beck's Natural Boneless Pork Loin

1 tsp black pepper

½ tsp salt

½ Copperhead Onion

- Place roast in pan; insert meat thermometer in thickest part.
- Sprinkle pepper and salt on roast.
- Slice onion; place on top of roast. Bake in 325 degree oven 2 hours, or until internal temperature of 160-170 degrees.
- Serves 6-8.

Cranberry Glazed Roast Pork

1 (4 lb) Beck's Pork Tenderloin or Boneless Roast

1 cup Sallie's Cranberry Chutney

1 tbsp chili sauce

2 tsp dry mustard

½ tsp salt

- Place roast on rack in open shallow pan; bake at 325 degrees 2-2½ hours.
- Mix together chutney, chili sauce, mustard and salt in small saucepan; simmer 3 minutes.
- Brush roast with sauce 30 minutes before pork is done, and again 10 minutes before removing from oven.
- Serve the remaining hot sauce with the roast.
- Serves 6-8.

Margarita Pork Chops

2 tbsp Saguaro Honey

3 tbsp soy sauce

4 tbsp Cahill Desert Products Margarita Marmalade

2 tbsp rice vinegar

½ cup Arizona Vineyards Blanc White Burgundy

6 pork chops

- Combine first 5 ingredients in saucepan; warm until sauce is smooth, stirring occasionally.
- Broil, bake or pan fry the pork chops, basting liberally until desired doneness.
- Serve with any remaining sauce.
- Serves 6.

Glazed Mesquite Smoked Ham

1 (8 oz) jar currant jelly
1 tbsp prepared mustard
¼ tsp cinnamon
¼ tsp crushed cloves
¼ cup pineapple juice
1 Beck's Mesquite Boneless Ham

- Combine first 5 ingredients; set aside.
- Place ham into shallow pan; score top side into diamond shapes. Insert meat thermometer.
- Pour half of jelly/mustard mixture over ham; cover with foil; cook at 325 degrees 20 minutes.
- Pour remaining ingredients on ham; cook until meat thermometer reaches 145 degrees; uncover for the last 20 minutes.
- Serves 10-12.

Roquefort Lamb Patties

2 lbs ground Arizona Lamb
1 tsp salt
¼ tsp ground pepper
2 medium onions, sliced
3 tbsp butter
3 tbsp crumbled Roquefort cheese
1 tbsp butter
1 tbsp chopped parsley
3 tsp all-purpose flour
½ cup Foremost® Sour Cream

- In medium bowl, mix lamb, salt and pepper. Shape into 6 patties.
- Broil 3″-4″ from source of heat, 3-5 minutes on each side, or until desired doneness.
- In small skillet, sauté onions in butter until soft; remove and keep warm.
- In small saucepan, mix together Roquefort, butter, parsley and flour; stir in sour cream.
- Heat and stir 1 minute, or until just warmed and slightly thickened.
- To serve, place sautéed onions on lamb patties; spoon Roquefort sauce on top.
- Serves 6.

Pistachio Lamb Meatballs in Indian Curry Sauce

1 lb ground Arizona Lamb

½ cup finely chopped The Arizona Pistachio Company Pistachios

1 egg

3 tbsp bread crumbs

¾ tsp grated lemon peel

¼ tsp Sahuaro Spice Co. Salt

¼ tsp Sahuaro Spice Co. Pepper

¼ tsp Sahuaro Spice Co. Cumin

2 tbsp vegetable oil

2 tbsp melted butter

1 cup chopped onions

2½ tsp curry powder

1½ tsp minced garlic

1 tbsp sugar

1 tbsp cornstarch

water

3 cups plain yogurt

hot cooked rice

chopped The Arizona Pistachio Company Pistachios

chopped fresh coriander

- Combine lamb, pistachios, egg, bread crumbs, lemon peel, salt, pepper and cumin; mix well.

- Shape into 1″ balls. In a sauté pan, brown meatballs lightly over medium heat in oil; remove from heat and drain on paper towels while preparing the sauce.

- In same pan, combine butter, onions, curry powder and garlic; cook until fragrant.

- In a separate bowl, combine sugar, cornstarch and enough water to make a smooth paste.

- Stir yogurt and sugar mixture into onions; heat slowly 10 minutes, stirring frequently. Pour sauce over meatballs.

- To serve, spoon meatballs and sauce over rice.

- Sprinkle with chopped pistachios and coriander.

- Serves 4-6.

Arizona Leg of Lamb

1 cup wine vinegar
1 cup vegetable oil
2 cloves Rhee's Garlic, whole
1 bay leaf, crumbled
2 tsp salt
1 tsp rosemary
1 tsp sage
½ tsp crushed pepper
1 (5-7 lb) boned, rolled and tied leg of lamb
3 large potatoes
3 Copperhead Onions, quartered
3 large chilies or peppers, sliced
2 Rhee's Garlic Bulbs, skin removed

- Combine vinegar, oil and seasonings; pour over lamb.
- Cover; marinate in refrigerator 12-24 hours, turning often.
- Remove lamb; strain marinade and reserve.
- Place potatoes, onions, chilies and garlic in shallow roasting pan; pour ¼ cup marinade over vegetables.
- Place lamb on roasting rack over vegetables; insert meat thermometer. Pour ¼ cup marinade over lamb. Roast at 325 degrees 25 minutes per lb, or until meat thermometer registers 140 degrees for rare or 150-155 degrees for medium.
- Baste with ¼ cup marinade every 20-30 minutes.
- Allow lamb to stand 15 minutes before carving; serve with vegetables.
- Use drippings for gravy, if desired, removing the garlic bulbs.
- Serves 8-10.

Lamb Loin Calvados

2, 1 lb loins of lamb, trimmed and tenderloin removed

2 tbsp vegetable oil

¼ cup Shamrock® Margarine

3 cups sliced fresh mushrooms

2 medium Valley's Finest Apples, seeded and sliced

½ cup calvados

¼ cup R. W. Webb Arizona Fume Blanc

1 cup Shamrock® Heavy Cream

2 tsp cinnamon

½ tsp salt

- In large ovenproof skillet, sear lamb loins in hot oil on all surfaces until well browned, about 5 minutes.
- Place skillet with lamb in 400 degree oven until medium, about 8-10 minutes. Remove lamb from skillet and keep warm.
- In same skillet, add margarine; sauté mushrooms and apples until soft. Remove and set aside; keep warm.
- Add calvados, wine, cream, cinnamon and salt to pan; simmer 15 minutes, or until thickened.
- To serve, spoon sauce on serving platter.
- Slice loins into ½" pieces. Place on sauce; top with mushrooms and apples.
- Serves 8.

Classic Rack of Lamb

1, 8 rib rack of lamb, well-trimmed

1½ tsp stone ground mustard

½ cup unseasoned dry bread crumbs

¼ cup snipped fresh Rhee's Parsley

½ tsp crushed dried rosemary leaves

¼ tsp black pepper

- On roasting rack in shallow baking pan, place lamb roast meaty side up; insert meat thermometer. Spread mustard over meat.
- Combine bread crumbs, parsley, rosemary and pepper.
- Pat bread crumb mixture into mustard. Roast at 375 degrees until desired doneness; 140 degrees for rare, 150-155 degrees for medium, or 160 degrees for medium well. Let roast stand 10 minutes before carving.
- Serves 4.

Rainbow Bridge near Lake Powell

Braised Lamb Shanks Provencal

4-5 Arizona Lamb Shanks

3 tbsp olive oil

1 onion, sliced

2 cloves garlic, mashed

1 (15 oz) can tomatoes, cut in pieces

1 cup R. W. Webb Arizona Fume Blanc

1 tbsp curry powder

1 tsp salt

½ tsp black pepper

1 orange rind, peeled in strips

1 eggplant, unpeeled, cut in 1" cubes

1 tbsp flour mixed with ¼ cup R. W. Webb Arizona Fume Blanc

½ (1 lb) pkg cooked Creamette® Medium Egg Noodles

- Brown lamb shanks in oil in large ovenproof casserole; remove.
- Brown onion and garlic in remaining oil, scraping pan to loosen browned meat juices.
- Add tomatoes, wine, curry powder, salt, pepper and orange rind. Heat to simmer; stir in eggplant cubes.
- Place browned lamb shanks on mixture. Cover casserole; simmer gently in 300-325 degree oven 2½ hours.
- Remove lamb and vegetables; place on serving platter. Discard orange rind.
- Thicken sauce in casserole pan by stirring in the flour and wine; cook over medium heat until thick. Adjust seasoning. Place sauce in gravy boat.
- Prepare noodles according to pkg directions; drain.
- Serve lamb and vegetables over hot noodles. Spoon generous amounts of sauce on top.
- Serves 4-5.

Grilled Chicken Breasts with Lime/Dill Sauce

4 Young's Farm Chicken Breast Halves,
deboned and skinned

Marinade:
¼ cup Fresh Pic Lime Juice
¼ tsp salt
⅛ tsp pepper
½ tsp dried dillweed
½ tsp dried minced onion
2 tbsp melted Shamrock® Butter
cooked Creamette® Wide Egg Noodles

- Combine all marinade ingredients in heavy zip-lock plastic bag; mix.
- Add chicken breasts; seal bag. Turn to coat chicken with marinade; let stand at room temperature 10-15 minutes.
- Meanwhile, preheat charcoal grill.
- Place chicken breasts over medium coals or low setting on gas grill. Cover; grill 5 minutes on each side.
- Baste with butter after turning.
- Serve hot with buttered noodles.
- Serves 4.

Chicken with Pistachio Sauce

2 whole Young's Farm Chicken Breasts,
skinned, halved and boned
⅛ tsp pepper
1 tbsp oil
½ cup Jackson Orange Juice
2 tbsp water
2 tsp lemon juice
½ tsp grated orange peel
2 tbsp sliced green onion
¼ cup chopped Arizona Nuts Pistachios

- Pound chicken breasts to ¼" thickness; season with pepper.
- Sauté in oil 2-3 minutes on each side.
- Add orange juice, water, lemon juice and orange peel.
- Simmer, covered, 10 minutes or until chicken is tender. Remove chicken.
- Add green onion to pan; cook over medium heat until slightly thickened. Pour over chicken.
- Sprinkle with pistachios.
- Serves 4.

Chicken Monterey

2 tbsp vegetable oil
6 boneless chicken breasts
2 tbsp Sonoran Seasoning
1 (12 oz) btl Prickly Pear
Barbecue Glaze
6 slices UDA Seal of Arizona Monterey
Jack Cheese
6 slices Bar-S Bacon, cooked

- Brush chicken liberally with oil and sprinkle with seasoning.
- Grill chicken over medium coals 10 minutes each side, or until done.
- Cover chicken with glaze, top with cheese and slice of bacon; cook until cheese begins to melt.
- Pour remaining glaze in serving dish and place chicken on top.
- Serves 6.

Lemon Sherry Chicken Breasts

¼ tsp black pepper
6 chicken breast halves, boned
and skinned
2 tbsp corn oil margarine
⅔ cup chicken bouillon
2 tbsp R. W. Webb Arizona Gold
Cortado Sherry
1 fresh Sunkist® Lemon, juiced and
peel grated
2 tsp cornstarch
1 cup evaporated skimmed milk
¼ cup grated Parmesan cheese

- Sprinkle pepper evenly over chicken breasts.
- In large skillet, bring margarine and chicken bouillon to boil.
- Add chicken breasts; cook over medium heat, turning once or twice, just until chicken is no longer pink, 6-10 minutes.
- Remove chicken from skillet; place in ovenproof serving dish.
- Add sherry, lemon juice and peel to mixture in skillet.
- Add cornstarch to milk; mix well with wire whisk.
- Gradually add to mixture in skillet, stirring constantly, until it comes to boil and thickens.
- Pour sauce over chicken.
- Sprinkle tops of chicken with Parmesan cheese; place under broiler until golden brown.
- Serves 6.

Curried Chicken Breasts

1 cup all-purpose flour
½ tsp salt
¼ tsp pepper
6 Young's Farm Chicken Breasts
4 tbsp Carnation® Butter
1 (10.75 oz) can mushroom soup
1 cup Carnation® Sour Cream
1 tsp curry powder
cooked rice

- Combine flour, salt and pepper.
- Dredge breasts in seasoned flour.
- Brown chickens in butter; put in casserole dish.
- Mix soup, sour cream and curry powder; pour over chicken.
- Bake, covered, 1 hour at 300 degrees.
- Serve with rice.
- Serves 6.

Honey Baked Chicken

⅓ cup melted UDA Seal of Arizona Butter
2 tbsp prepared mustard
⅓ cup Mountain Top Honey
1 tsp salt
1 tsp curry powder
1 (3 lb) Young's Farm Frying Chicken, cut up and skinned

- Combine first 5 ingredients; pour over chicken.
- Bake 1¼ hours at 350 degrees, basting every 15 minutes until chicken is tender and evenly browned.
- Serves 6.

Honey Lemon Chicken

⅓ cup all-purpose flour
1 tsp paprika
1 tsp salt
1 (2½-3 lb) chicken, skinned and cut into pieces
⅓ cup melted butter
⅓ cup Malcolm's Honey
¼ cup Sunkist® Lemon Juice

- Combine flour, paprika and salt.
- Roll chicken in flour mixture.
- Drizzle butter over floured pieces of chicken.
- Bake at 375 degrees 40-45 minutes.
- Reduce heat to 350 degrees.
- Mix honey and lemon juice.
- Baste chicken with honey mixture every 5 minutes for 15 minutes additional baking.
- Serves 4-6.

Crunchy Fried Chicken

1 (2-3 lb) fryer chicken
1½ cups finely chopped The Pecan Store Pecans
1 cup all-purpose flour
1 cup Silver Creek Mill Yellow Corn Meal
2 tsp salt
2 tsp black pepper
2 tsp cayenne
4 Laid in Arizona Eggs
½ cup melted butter
4 cups vegetable oil

- Cut up chicken into pieces, wash well and dry slightly.
- Combine all dry ingredients in a bowl; mix well.
- In another bowl, mix eggs and butter. Dip chicken pieces into the liquid mixture, then toss in dry mixture to coat thoroughly. Repeat this step for thick coated chicken.
- Heat oil in large, deep skillet; add chicken pieces a few at a time.
- Fry 10-12 minutes on each side.
- Drain on paper towels or a rack.
- Serves 4-6.

Asian Peppered Chicken

8 chicken thighs
2 tbsp fresh minced garlic
2 tbsp fresh grated ginger
1 bunch cilantro, with roots
1½ tsp Santa Cruz Coarse Ground Black Pepper
6 tbsp Cinnabar Asian Tamarind Sauce

- Wash, skin and prick thighs with a knife tip or skewer.
- Chop garlic, ginger and cilantro; combine.
- Add pepper to dry marinade.
- Toss with chicken in a bowl to coat; refrigerate 2-4 hours.
- Grill over charcoal 5 minutes. Start basting with tamarind sauce. The chicken will take on a mahogany brown color. Turn and baste frequently.
- Grill 15 minutes.
- Serves 4.

Chicken Barbecue

1 (3 lb) Young's Farm Chicken, cut up
3 tbsp vegetable oil
¼ cup Sonoran Seasoning
1 (12 oz) btl Prickly Pear Barbecue Glaze

- Oil and liberally sprinkle seasoning on chicken.
- Grill over medium coals, 15-20 minutes each side, or until done.
- Brush glaze over chicken and grill 2 minutes.
- Serve with remaining glaze.
- Serves 6.

Jamaican Jerk Spiced Rock Cornish Hens

2 (1 lb) Rock Cornish hens
3 tbsp Cinnabar Jerk Spice
3 tbsp vegetable oil
cooked rice
French bread

- Skin and wash the game hens.
- Cut down the back on either side of the backbone and remove. Spread hen out with palm of hand to flatten. Score meat lightly with a knife.
- Mix spice with vegetable oil in shallow pan; place hens in marinade. Massage spice into meat with your fingers.
- Place pan in refrigerator overnight. The longer the marination, the hotter the flavor.
- Light a charcoal fire.
- Cook hens very slowly 1 hour, or until done.
- Baste with remaining marinade. Long and slow cooking will keep the meat moist.
- Serve with Jamaican Dirty Rice (recipe on page 170), white rice or hot French bread.
- Serves 2.

Chicken with Pecans

½ cup melted UDA Seal of Arizona Butter

1 tbsp chopped onion

½ cup chopped Country Estate Pecans

2 cups bread crumbs

⅛ tsp ground pepper

⅓ cup chopped celery

¼ tsp salt

¼ cup water

4 chicken breasts, seasoned with salt and pepper

additional melted butter

- In bowl, pour butter over all ingredients except chicken. The stuffing should not be too moist.
- Arrange 4 mounds of stuffing in greased casserole.
- Place chicken breasts, skin side up, on top of each mound of stuffing. Brush with additional melted butter.
- Cover with foil; bake in preheated 350 degree oven 45 minutes.
- Remove foil; bake 15 minutes longer, or until brown.
- Serves 4.

Thai Satay with Peanut Sauce

12" bamboo skewers, presoaked in water

1 lb beef, pork or chicken, very thinly sliced and cut into strips 1" wide and 4" long

½ lime, juiced

½ tbsp vegetable oil

4 tbsp Cinnabar Thai Seafood Marinade

8 tbsp crunchy peanut butter

1 small yellow onion, finely chopped

1 cup thick coconut milk (put can of coconut milk in freezer for 15 minutes and spoon the thickest from the top of the opened can)

4 tbsp Cinnabar Thai Seafood Marinade

- Thread the sliced meat ribbon-style onto the skewers and lay in shallow pan.
- Mix the next 3 ingredients; pour on meat. Marinate for 1 hour, turning skewers frequently.
- Light a very hot charcoal fire.
- Heat peanut butter, onion, coconut milk and Thai marinade in saucepan; bring to boil. Remove from heat.
- Take skewers from marinade; cook as quickly as possible over a very hot fire. Time will depend on how thin you have sliced the meat but should never exceed 3 or 4 minutes.
- Serve immediately with the sauce on the side.
- Serves 6.

Beer Bar-B-Que Turkey Steaks

1 pkg (8 filets) Young's Farm Turkey Steaks, ⅜" thick

Sallie's Saltmix

1 cup Big Horn Premium Ale Beer

1 tbsp brown sugar

⅛ tsp hot pepper sauce

1 onion, chopped

1 tbsp vegetable oil

salt and pepper

- Rub turkey with seasoning salt; place in baking dish.
- Mix remaining ingredients; pour over turkey.
- Cover; refrigerate at least 4 hours.
- Drain and reserve marinade.
- Grill, brushing with marinade.
- Pan fry 2 minutes on each side.
- Cook until turkey is light gold in color.
- Serves 4-6.

Turkey Kebabs

¼ cup sugar

½ cup dry sherry

¼ cup soy sauce

1 (1¼ lb) pkg Young's Farm Turkey Chunks

2 small Young's Farm Zucchini

½ cup pineapple chunks

2 Copperhead Onions, quartered

salt and pepper

- Mix sugar, sherry and soy sauce in 1 qt saucepan.
- Cook over medium heat, stirring until sugar dissolves, cool.
- Place turkey chunks in glass dish; pour mixture over turkey.
- Cover; refrigerate at least 3 hours, turning occasionally. Drain turkey, save marinade.
- Alternate chunks of turkey, zucchini, pineapple and onions on skewers; brush with marinade.
- Grill until done.
- Sprinkle with salt and pepper.
- Serves 4-5.

Baked Tilapia

4 tilapia filets
4 tsp Carnation® Butter
½ cup mushroom soup
⅓ cup sherry
¼ cup sliced mushrooms
dash Worcestershire sauce
chopped Rhee's Parsley

- In saucepan, brown filets in butter.
- Remove filets and place in greased baking pan; cover with mushroom soup and sherry.
- Sprinkle with mushrooms, Worcestershire sauce and parsley.
- Bake 20-25 minutes at 350 degrees.
- Serves 4.

Pistachio Steamed Halibut

4 halibut steaks
salt and pepper
3 lemon slices
water
½ cup sliced celery
¼ cup diagonally sliced green onions
1 tbsp vegetable oil
1 cup chopped Pavo Roma Tomato
¼ tsp crushed thyme
¼ cup chopped, shelled Arizona Nuts Pistachios

- Season halibut with salt and pepper; top each steak with lemon slice.
- Put steaks on heat-proof plate; place on rack over ½" simmering water in skillet.
- Cover and steam 10 minutes per 1" of thickness, or until fish flakes easily when tested with fork.
- Sauté celery and green onions in oil; add tomato and thyme; heat thoroughly.
- Add pistachios; mix well.
- Spoon over halibut steaks.
- Serves 4.

Guido's Shrimp Marinara

1 (14 oz) pkg De Cio Pasta Sweet Bell
Pepper, Rafaela's Herb or Spinach Basil
Garlic Pasta
2 tbsp butter
3 tbsp olive oil
2 cloves garlic, chopped
1 large onion, julienned
1 large Pavo Bell Pepper, julienned
2 carrots, julienned
½ cup sliced mushrooms
½ cup Arizona Vineyards Workers
Red Wine
1 tbsp basil
1 (32 oz) can Italian tomatoes
1 (6 oz) can tomato sauce
1 tbsp brown sugar
1 cup cooked and cleaned shrimp

- Cook pasta according to pkg directions.
- Melt butter into oil over low heat.
- Add garlic, onion, pepper, carrots and mushrooms. Sauté until onions and peppers are soft.
- Turn heat to medium; add wine, bring to boil.
- Add basil, tomatoes with juice, tomato sauce and brown sugar.
- Bring to boil again; simmer 20 minutes.
- Add cooked shrimp, simmer 2 minutes.
- Serve over cooked pasta.
- Serves 6-8.

Salmon Loaf

1 (16 oz) can salmon
1 egg, beaten
½ cup Shamrock® Cream
3 tbsp melted Shamrock® Butter
2 tbsp Arizona Southwest Mix
1 tbsp lemon juice
1 cup bread crumbs
⅛ tsp pepper

- Combine all ingredients; place in buttered 8″ x 4″ loaf pan.
- Bake at 350 degrees 30 minutes.
- Serves 4-6.

Fish Filets with Pineapple-Pistachio Sauce

2 cups unsweetened pineapple juice

dash cayenne

1/4 cup plain lowfat yogurt

6 white fish filets

1/4 cup coarsely chopped Arizona Nuts Pistachios

1 1/2 tbsp chopped fresh chives or green onion

- Preheat oven to 375 degrees.
- Combine pineapple juice and cayenne. Bring to boil; boil gently until reduced to 2/3 cup, 15-20 minutes.
- Remove pan from heat; whisk in yogurt.
- Lightly oil baking dish. Place filets in dish; cover with foil.
- Bake until fish is opaque, 6-10 minutes.
- Just before serving, reheat sauce, but do not boil.
- Stir in pistachios and chives or onion.
- Spoon sauce over fish.
- Serves 6.

GRAZING ARIZONA

"Arizona is one vast grazing ground. Except a strip of country along the Great river [Colorado] and a portion of that region north of the Little Colorado, there is no part of the Territory without a growth of grass."
—*Resources of Arizona*, 1884

Spanish and Mexican ranchers began in the eighteenth century to graze their cattle in the valleys of the San Pedro and Santa Cruz rivers. Periodic Apache raids forced the ranchers to abandon their ranches, first along the remote San Pedro, then along the more settled Santa Cruz south of Tucson.

The abandoned bulls grew wild and mean, and that led to one of the oddest episodes in Arizona history.

As the Mormon Battalion marched westward in 1846, it encountered some of the wild bulls along the San Pedro, near the site of present-day Benson. The bulls attacked the wagons and gored the mules. Several men were injured. The battle raged for several hours, while soldiers killed dozens of bulls. Some of the tough old animals staggered off, still alive, with a several musket balls in them. The fray was the battalion's only "battle" en route to California.

After the United States acquired Arizona from Mexico, it took more than two decades for the territory's legendary grazing industry to catch on. Historian Jay Wagoner, an authority on Arizona ranching history, says the ubiquitous Bill Kirkland was the first Anglo to raise cattle here. He brought 200 head of Mexican cattle north to the old Canoa Spanish land grant near Tucson in 1857. Kirkland was one of the men who raised the flag over Tucson in 1856. He built the first home in Phoenix, and later ranched in a northern Arizona valley that bears his name.

Resources of Arizona listed the outstanding qualities of several varieties of grass found here. "This grass grows from one end of Arizona to the other. . . The quality of beef made from it is unequaled for tenderness and flavor. No such meat is raised anywhere in the United States, and travelers are enthusiastic when discussing a juicy steak or a tender roast grown on the native grasses of Arizona."

That's clearly promotional hype, but there was taller grass here in the 1870s and 1880s than Arizona ranchers have seen in the several generations since. The mild climate, which made year-round ranching possible, also meant that once grazed, grasses did not regenerate like grasses in wetter climates. Ranchers immediately had to adjust the number of animals downward, and they have been adjusting ever since.

Henry C. Hooker trailed large herds of Texas longhorns to southeastern Arizona in the 1870s to supply beef to Army posts and the contractors who supplied Indian reservations. Hooker soon controlled a vast area of public grazing lands. The town of Willcox was established on the Southern Pacific Railroad near Hooker's headquarters as a shipping point for cattle. Some years later Willcox became the hometown of cowboy singer Rex Allen, and it's still a cowboy's kind of town.

John H. Slaughter, model for the TV series "Sheriff of Cochise," did indeed clean up Cochise County between 1887 and 1890. He was, after all, a former Texas Ranger.

Slaughter leased, then bought, the 70,000-acre San Bernardino Ranch in Arizona and Mexico. He ran 30,000 head of cattle. He irrigated 500 acres of grain and vegetables with water from artesian wells. The dining room of his sprawling hacienda-style home was a favorite with visiting dignitaries. The San Bernardino Ranch is now a national historic landmark and a museum open to the public.

Slaughter's second cousin, Pete Slaughter, brought Herefords into the White Mountains of east-central Arizona. His P.S. Ranch was on a much smaller scale than John Slaughter's outfit. Numerically, most ranches in Arizona were smaller ones. A ranch usually has a small base of privately-owned land, from which the owner spreads out onto federal and state grazing leases.

But some of the big spreads helped make Arizona famous as cattle country. Aztec Land & Cattle Company owned the notorious "Hashknife Outfit" in northern Arizona, so named because its brand resembled a popular tool in kitchens and chuckwagons. The Hashknife controlled two million acres north of the Mogollon Rim, and ran 50,000 cattle and 2,000 horses. It was so large, and for a time so carelessly run, that it employed some genuinely bad guys. We'll get back to that part of the Arizona legend later.

North and west of the Hashknife, Babbitt Brothers owned the CO-Bar. It started with 1,200 head, and got bigger over several decades. It's generally accepted that some neighboring ranchers, including former Babbitt cowboys, got their start helping themselves to Babbit stock. The Babbitts became partners in ranches scattered throughout Arizona and at one time controlled some large spreads. Those holdings were gradually shed, but the CO-Bar is still in business northeast of Flagstaff.

Two sons of Mormon President Brigham Young also started large cattle outfit in the Flagstaff area in the 1880s. And up in the Arizona Strip, a ranch house called Windsor Castle, another Mormon establishment, was built like a fortress. It is today Pipe Spring National Monument. In appropriate seasons, park employes and local volunteers get themselves up in pioneer garb and do living history demonstrations of branding, roping, cooking, churning, sewing.

Apache and Navajo tribes run large tribal cattle herds. And ranching even extends over into the western parts of Arizona, where grass is thinner and water scarcer. They tell of one rancher along the Big Sandy River in Mohave County who had to take down one of his windmills; there wasn't enough wind for two.

Phoenix was a farm town, not a cow town, a matter of some disappointment to today's romantics and would-be cowboys. Still, it was a trade center for much of Arizona's ranching. The historic Adams Hotel and its Cattlemen's Bar were headquarters for the industry for a long time.

In the fall of 1909, after roundup, rancher Al Kellogg rode in from his ranch at Bloody Basin and found himself starring in a scene right out of a John Wayne movie. A "dope fiend" named William McMahon had been terrorizing downtown Phoenix with a razor. He cut a policeman and a mine promoter.

Riding his horse along Center Street in front of the Adams, Kellogg shook a loop in his lariat, roped the dope fiend and dragged him along the dusty street until he dropped the razor.

Arizona also supported a sizeable sheep industry. Manuel Candelaria started it in the 1860s when he drove a large band of sheep from New Mexico to the area of Concho in present-day Apache County. John Clark and the three Daggs brothers ran sheep in the Flagstaff and Snowflake areas. Eventually, the Babbitt brothers got into raising sheep, that are reputed to have bleated, "Ba-abbitt." Sheepmen and cattlemen were not always compatible, for simple economic reasons. Cattlemen claimed sheep cropped the grass too close, ruining the range for cattle.

Hashknife cowboys drove sheep off the range, and brutalized herders. It is said that Daggs brothers sheep, driven south over the Mogollon Rim into Pleasant Valley after the Hashknife ran them off, ignited a feud that killed at least thirty people in the 1880s and 1890s. The Pleasant Valley War was also called the Graham-Tewksbury feud, with Tewksburys favoring sheep and the Grahams defending their cattle ranch. However, author Don Dedera, who studied the war for thirty years, concluded its causes were nowhere near that simple; sheep triggered a more complicated grudge fight.

In the 1880s, ranchers began trailing sheep north in the spring from the Salt River and Gila valleys to the forests in the north, then trailing them back in the fall. The trip, over well-established sheep trails, sometimes took two months. Many of the herders, and later some of the ranchers, were Basques from the Pyrenees.

For better or for worse, much of Arizona's wild and woolly reputation came not from the ranchers, but from the hired hands of the cattle spreads, the cowboys. Some of them were quiet, thoughtful men like the character novelist Owen Wister called "The Virginian."

Others were cold, footloose criminals. At some times and some places in Arizona, the epithet "cowboy" did not mean a drover, but an outlaw. The towns of Charleston and Galeyville near Tombstone were heavily populated with outlaws; so was Springerville.

The Clantons, who faced the Earps and Doc Holliday at the O.K. Corral, owned a ranch outside Springerville. Legend says they sold cattle and horses stolen from southern Arizona in the Springerville country, then turned around and stole more stock to drive back south. Ike Clanton, a career cattle thief, was gunned down south of Springerville in 1888 by a "range deputy" carrying a detective's badge he had earned from a correspondence school. The deputy sent Ike's brother Phin to Yuma Territorial Prison.

Cattle rustling became so common that thieves began to believe they were in a legitimate business. In southern Arizona, the term "cowboys" was applied to organized bands of rustlers, robbers and highwaymen. Things got so bad that President Chester A. Arthur issued a vaguely-worded proclamation threatening to clean up Arizona lawlessness with federal troops if the Territory didn't take care of its problems. The threat came to naught.

In 1901, the Arizona Rangers were formed to deal with rustlers. Captain Burton Mossman, a former Texas Ranger, had been hired as superintendent to clean up the Hashknife Outfit. He was recruited as the first of several men to captain the highly successful rangers. The TV series "Twenty-six Men" was based on the hard life of the rangers. They worked statewide, but their headquarters was in Cochise County, where much of the lawlessness was centered along the Mexican border.

Obviously, a lot of Arizona's cowboys were ordinary fellows working for a living. They had to know a little bit about a lot of things: building fences, doctoring stock, fixing pumps, knowing how to "read" grass and weather. Some of them became owners of small ranches all around the state. Many of these cowhands and ranchers competed in the "cowboy tournaments" that became popular in the 1880s and eventually were called "rodeos." Prescott has registered the trademark of its Frontier Days rodeo, which began in 1888, and also registered the slogan "World's Oldest Rodeo." Everett Bowman, who had a small ranch southwest of Prescott, was the first president of the Cowboy Turtle Association, today's Professional Rodeo Cowboys Association.

Payson's more rustic summer rodeo, which began in the same era as the Prescott contest, is another must-experience event for fans of Arizona cowboys.

And then there were the showman-type cowboys, like Tom Horn and Arizona Charlie Meadows. Meadows' father and brother were killed when Indians raided the family ranch near Payson in 1882, running off some of the livestock. Not long after, Meadows and Horn began competing in the tournaments, and in impromptu events at Phoenix, Globe and Prescott, frequently drawing side bets on their personal contest to be Arizona's champion cowboy.

The vainglorious Meadows became an expert roper and rider, a crack shot, a skilled swordsman and an expert with the bull whip. He toured the United States, New Zealand and Australia with his own shows or with other shows. He appeared in Chicago and London with William F. "Buffalo Bill" Cody's wild west show.

Another competitor at Prescott was movie cowboy Tom Mix, who in 1913 was grand marshall and won the bull riding event. Mix was killed in an auto accident near Florence, Arizona in 1940, and a monument beside U.S. 89 marks the site of his death. Part-time Arizonans like Mix, and natives like Rex Allen and Marty Robbins, didn't hurt the state's cowboy legend. Neither did a lot of cowboy movies filmed here, beginning with silent Cisco Kid movies filmed from 1913 to 1915.

There are several false-fronted, informal "cowboy" steakhouses around Arizona. In some, anyone who is audacious enough to wear a necktie will find it cut off with scissors and stapled to a rafter. And if you order a steak well-done, you're likely to be presented a dried-up old cowboy boot on a platter.

A "cowboy steak" is usually a large T-bone. The "cowgirl" portion is likely a porterhouse. They're broiled over mesquite charcoal, naturally.

In real life, a cowboy only saw such steak on payday, when he got to Holbrook or Willcox. What he ate on the range, if he was lucky, was a piece of round steak floured and fried in grease in an open dutch oven. And if he was really fortunate, the cook would tenderize the meat with an axe or a claw hammer before he fried it.

C.J. Babbitt, one of the men memorialized in Dean Smith's 1989 biography *Brothers Five*, told it this way: "We did our own cooking and ate our own beef, except on roundups, when we tried to eat everybody else's. On the winter range, one of the main chores was 'riding the river,' the Little Colorado, to look for bogged-down cows. We slept on quilts with wool blankets on top and tarps all around. In winter the men lived in a tent without a stove, and the menu was pretty limited—dried fruit, white beans, beef, sow belly, condensed milk, biscuits and coffee."

The menu got so monotonous that some cattlemen found ways to swap for mutton and lamb.

As with everything else in Arizona, ranching has changed a lot since World War II. Physically, it has probably gotten easier, with better roads and new equipment.

But it is increasingly hard for a rancher to put together the needed grazing land. Some of the better ranches have become investments for physicians or movie stars like the late John Wayne, who was a partner in two Arizona ranches. Patented land is going for more profitable uses, such as subdivisions, and the administrators of public land are under increasing pressure from environmentalists. Red tape gets stickier at all levels. A rancher has to pay a lot more attention to sophisticated breeding, marketing and bookkeeping practices.

Cattle feeding, long practiced in Arizona, became a major part of the industry in the irrigated valleys. What it lacked in glamour, it made up for in efficiency.

One innovative agriculturalist, Elmer Young, has since 1946 turned his place into a profitable business and a popular tourist attraction. Young's Farm is at Dewey, between Phoenix and Prescott. It sits beside Arizona Highway 69, which in earlier days was the primary Phoenix-Prescott stagecoach route.

Young's Farm and its meat processing plant provide custom-finished beef and hogs to buyers who are picky about quality and freshness. The country store also sells a lot of poultry and produce.

In late summer, city-dwellers set out to Young's Farm for fresh sweet corn raised there in the Verde Valley a few miles away. Sweet corn is also a prime cash crop in Chino Valley, historic ranching country north of Prescott.

For all the changes in ranching, an amazing number of ranchers large and small are preserving the old lifestyle in Arizona. To hear a rancher tell it, he has never seen less grass, less rain, or lower prices than right now, but those drawbacks have never stopped them.

Walking along main street in some small town—St. Johns or Florence—you'll see a bowlegged fellow with eyes faded about the same color as his six-year-old Levi's. His hat is as battered as his face, but he may be wearing $1,000, handmade boots of kiwi hide.

Cattlemen say that such a rancher stopped in a convenience store in Springerville to buy a ticket in the Arizona lottery. Someone asked him what he would do if he won.

"Oh, I'd just keep ranchin' until it was all gone," he replied.

PASTA

The Little Colorado River near Cameron

Spaghetti Primavera

1 tbsp olive oil

2 medium zucchini, sliced

2 cups sliced fresh mushrooms

1 medium Pavo Green Bell Pepper, julienned

1 (28 oz) can whole tomatoes, undrained and cut up

2 (6 oz) cans tomato paste

1 cup sliced, pitted ripe olives

1 tsp salt

½ tsp basil leaves

¼ tsp pepper

¼ cup grated Parmesan cheese

1 (1 lb) pkg Creamette® Thin Spaghetti or Vermicelli, uncooked

2 tbsp butter, softened

grated Parmesan cheese

- In large skillet, heat oil.
- Add zucchini, mushrooms and green pepper; cook until crisp tender.
- Stir in tomatoes, tomato paste, olives, salt, basil and pepper; bring to boil.
- Reduce heat; simmer 15 minutes.
- Stir in cheese.
- Prepare pasta according to pkg directions; drain.
- Add softened butter; toss to coat.
- Arrange on warm serving platter. Top with vegetable mixture and Parmesan cheese; serve immediately.
- Serves 8-10.

Green Chile Pasta

1 (10 oz) pkg Ladson's Fettuccine

2 cups sour cream

2 (4 oz) cans chopped green chilies

¾ cup grated Monterey Jack cheese

Sallie's Seasoning Salt

2 tbsp chopped Fresh Touch Gardens Chives

- Cook pasta according to pkg directions.
- Grease 9" x 13" pan.
- Layer ingredients in this order: pasta, sour cream, green chilies, cheese, salt and chives; repeat, ending with cheese and chives.
- Bake at 300 degrees 45 minutes.
- Serves 8-10.

Stir-Fry Mostaccioli

½ (1 lb) pkg Creamette® Mostaccioli,
uncooked

3 tbsp peanut oil

½ medium Pavo Red Bell Pepper,
julienned

½ medium Pavo Yellow Bell Pepper,
julienned

½ small red onion, cut into wedges

1 clove Rhee's Garlic, minced

¼ lb fresh snow peas

⅓ cup cashews

½ cup chicken broth

1 tsp cornstarch

½ tsp soy sauce

¼ tsp salt

dash ground ginger

- Prepare mostaccioli according to pkg directions; drain.
- In medium skillet, heat oil.
- Add peppers, onion and garlic; stir-fry 1 minute.
- Add snow peas; stir-fry until vegetables are crisp tender.
- Add mostaccioli and cashews; mix well.
- In small bowl, blend chicken broth, cornstarch, soysauce, salt and ginger; add to mostaccioli mixture.
- Cook and stir until sauce thickens.
- Arrange on warm serving platter; serve immediately.
- Serves 4-6.

Chile Alfredo

1 (8 oz) pkg Territorial Gourmet Red
Chile Pasta

½ cup Southwest Chile Pecans

Alfredo Sauce:

¼ cup melted Shamrock® Butter

¼ cup grated Parmesan cheese

2 tbsp Shamrock® Half and Half

¼ tsp salt

⅛ tsp pepper

- Prepare pasta according to pkg directions; drain and keep warm.
- In warm serving dish, combine sauce ingredients.
- Add noodles; toss with sauce to coat well.
- Sprinkle with pecans just before serving.
- Serves 4.

Red Wine Stroganoff

2 lbs sirloin, cubed

3 onions, chopped

5 cloves Rhee's Garlic, chopped

4 bay leaves

1 cup Carnation® Butter

½ (750 ml) btl Arizona Vineyards Workers Red Wine

1 tsp coriander

1 tbsp brown sugar

½ cup julienned carrots

½ tsp thyme

¼ tsp rosemary

½ tsp sage

½ cup Carnation® Heavy Cream

1 tbsp pepper

salt

1 (10 oz) pkg Ladson's Lemon Pepper Noodles, cooked

- Braise sirloin, onions, garlic and bay leaves in butter in large skillet until meat browns.
- Add wine, coriander and brown sugar; simmer 15-20 minutes.
- Add carrot, thyme, rosemary and sage; mix well.
- Add cream; simmer 1 hour.
- Add pepper and salt to taste; add more wine to taste.
- Serve over noodles.
- Serves 6-8.

Lasagne Giovanni

8 oz Creamette® Lasagne

1 lb ground beef

½ cup chopped onion

1 (15.5 oz) jar spaghetti sauce with mushrooms

1 tsp garlic salt

1 tsp crushed oregano

½ tsp crushed basil

1½ cups Foremost® Cottage Cheese

2 cups shredded Monterey Jack cheese

¾ cup grated Parmesan cheese

- Preheat oven to 350 degrees.
- Prepare lasagne according to pkg directions; drain.
- In large skillet, brown beef and onion; drain.
- Stir in spaghetti sauce, garlic salt, oregano and basil.
- In a 2 qt buttered rectangular baking dish, layer ⅓ of lasagne, ⅓ of sauce and ⅓ of cheeses. Repeat twice.
- Bake 30 minutes, or until hot and bubbly.
- Let stand 10 minutes before cutting.
- Serves 6-8.

Zucchini Lasagne

1 lb mild Schreiner's Italian Sausage,
casing removed

½ cup chopped onion

1 (15 oz) can tomato sauce

½ cup water

¼ tsp salt

¼ tsp oregano

¾ cup grated Parmesan cheese

2 tbsp all-purpose flour

8 Ladson's Lasagne Noodles, cooked
and drained

4 cups zucchini slices, cut ¼" thick

12 oz sliced UDA Seal of Arizona
Mozzarella Cheese

- Brown sausage with onion; drain.
- Stir in tomato sauce, water and seasonings. Simmer, uncovered, 30 minutes, stirring occasionally.
- Preheat oven to 375 degrees.
- Combine Parmesan cheese and flour.
- Layer half of lasagne noodles on bottom of buttered 13" x 9" baking dish.
- Layer over noodles in order, ½ zucchini, Parmesan mixture, meat sauce and mozzarella cheese.
- Repeat layers of noodles, zucchini, Parmesan mixture and meat sauce.
- Bake 20-25 minutes or until zucchini is tender.
- Add remaining mozzarella cheese; return to oven until cheese begins to melt.
- Let stand 10 minutes before serving.
- Serves 6.

Italian Casserole

½ (1 lb) pkg Creamette® Fettuccine

1 lb Schreiner's Fine Sausage Sweet or
Hot Italian Sausage

¼ cup chopped onion

1 (4 oz) can sliced mushrooms,
undrained

2 tbsp chopped pimento-stuffed olives

2 cups shredded UDA Seal of Arizona
Cheddar Cheese, divided

1 (8 oz) jar Territorial Gourmet Olé
Pasta Sauce

grated Parmesan cheese

- Preheat oven to 350 degrees.
- Prepare fettuccine according to pkg directions; drain.
- Remove sausage from casing; cook with onion in skillet over low heat until browned, breaking sausage into small pieces; drain.
- Toss together fettuccine, sausage, onion, mushrooms, olives, 1¾ cups Cheddar cheese and pizza sauce.
- Turn into casserole; bake 20-25 minutes or until cheese melts and casserole is heated thoroughly.
- Sprinkle with remaining Cheddar and Parmesan cheeses for last 10 minutes of baking.
- Serves 4-6.

Pasta with Clam Sauce

1 (14 oz) pkg De Cio Pasta
Spinach Basil Garlic, Beet Onion
or Ginger Carrot Pasta
3 tbsp olive oil
1 medium onion, chopped
2 cloves Rhee's Garlic, chopped fine
½ cup chopped Rhee's Parsley
¼ tsp grated ginger
16 oz clam juice
4 (6 oz) cans baby clams
salt and freshly ground pepper
grated Parmesan cheese

- Cook pasta according to pkg directions.
- For sauce, strain clams; reserve juice; set aside.
- In large frying pan, sauté oil, onion and garlic on low heat until onion is soft and transparent.
- Add parsley; sauté for 1 more minute.
- Add ginger and clam juice, including reserved clam juice.
- Bring sauce to boil 8-10 minutes; add clams, salt and pepper.
- Continue to cook on low heat 1 minute more.
- Serve over pasta and sprinkle with Parmesan cheese.
- Serves 4.

Party-Fare Pistachio Pasta

½ (1 lb) pkg Creamette® Spaghetti
1 clove garlic, minced
¼ cup chopped onion
2 tbsp olive oil or butter
½ cup coarsely chopped, Arizona Nuts Pistachios
¼ cup chopped ripe olives
¼ cup minced parsley
1 tsp lemon juice
⅛ tsp pepper
⅛ tsp crushed basil
¼ cup grated Parmesan cheese

- Prepare spaghetti according to pkg directions; drain.
- Sauté garlic and onion in oil until onion is tender.
- Add remaining ingredients, except cheese.
- Toss together; heat 2 minutes.
- Toss with Parmesan cheese.
- Serves 6-8 as appetizer.

Pasta Alfredo

1 (14 oz) pkg De Cio Pasta Tomato Basil
Garlic or Sweet Bell Pepper Pasta,
cooked and drained

6 tbsp unsalted butter

⅔ cup Foremost® Whipping Cream

½ tsp salt

large pinch white pepper

¼ tsp nutmeg

1 cup freshly grated Parmesan cheese

3 tbsp chopped fresh parsley

- Place butter and cream in 10″ skillet over medium heat.
- Cook, stirring constantly, until blended and mixture bubbles 2 minutes.
- Stir in salt, pepper and nutmeg; remove from heat.
- Gradually stir in Parmesan cheese until thoroughly blended and fairly smooth.
- Do not let sauce bubble.
- Pour sauce over pasta and place pot over low heat.
- Stir and toss gently with fork until pasta is slightly coated, 2-3 minutes.
- Sprinkle with parsley; serve immediately.
- Serve over cooked pasta.
- Serves 4-6.

Pasta in Herb Sauce

1 (14 oz) pkg De Cio Pasta Carrot-
Thyme or Lemon-Mint Pasta

¼ cup butter

½ cup olive oil

4 large cloves garlic, pressed

2 tbsp dry Sahuaro Spice Co. Basil

1 tbsp Sahuaro Spice Co. Fennel Seed

2 tsp parsley

¼ cup lemon juice

grated Parmesan cheese

- Melt butter into oil over low heat; add garlic.
- Add basil, fennel seed and parsley.
- Bring to medium heat, stirring constantly, 2-3 minutes; let simmer.
- Add lemon juice; heat 1 minute longer.
- Serve over cooked pasta.
- Sprinkle with Parmesan cheese.
- Serves 4-6.

Herb Pasta

5 tbsp butter, divided
1½ tbsp Arizona Herbal Spice Dip Mix
¼ lb fresh mushrooms, sliced
3 tbsp freshly grated Parmesan cheese
½ lb De Cio Pasta Mixed Tagliarini Confetti, cooked al dente and drained

- Melt 4 tbsp butter in heavy skillet over low heat; add dip mix and blend well.
- Remove from heat and let steep.
- Melt remaining butter; sauté mushrooms until tender.
- Combine all ingredients in large serving dish, sprinkle with cheese and serve immediately.
- Serves 4.

Manicotti Florentine

½ lb Barone Italian Sausage
1 (10 oz) pkg frozen spinach, thawed and well drained
1 cup Shamrock® Cottage Cheese
1 egg, beaten
1 clove garlic, minced
½ tsp crushed dried oregano
¼ tsp salt
dash pepper
1 (8 oz) pkg Creamette Manicotti, cooked and drained
1 (8 oz) can tomato sauce
½ cup shredded mozzarella cheese
2 tbsp grated Parmesan cheese

- Preheat oven to 350 degrees.
- Remove sausage from casing; crumble. Brown sausage; drain.
- Add spinach, cottage cheese, egg and seasonings; mix lightly.
- Fill each shell generously with sausage mixture.
- Place in 10" x 6" baking dish.
- Pour tomato sauce over shells. Sprinkle cheeses on top.
- Bake 25 minutes, or until thoroughly heated.
- Serves 4-6.

Pasta with Garden-Fresh Pistachio Cream Sauce

1 cup cream
½ cup tightly packed, chopped fresh Rhee's Basil Leaves
¼ tsp salt
⅛ tsp white pepper
¾ cup coarsely chopped The Arizona Pistachio Company Pistachios, divided
½ (1 lb) pkg Creamette® Fettuccine
½ cup julienned carrots
½ cup julienned zucchini
¼ cup water

- Combine cream, basil, salt and pepper in microwave bowl.
- Place in microwave; cook on MEDIUM 15 minutes, or until mixture is thickened and slightly reduced.
- Remove from microwave; stir in ½ cup pistachios and set aside.
- Prepare fettuccine according to pkg directions; drain.
- Place 2 connected white paper towels on counter.
- Spoon carrots and zucchini directly over perforation center. Fold over both sides and the ends to enclose vegetables.
- Place on microwave plate, perforated side up.
- Pour water over towel to moisten.
- Place in microwave; cook on HIGH 2 minutes.
- Carefully pull open perforation.
- Add carrots and zucchini to cream sauce.
- Spoon over hot cooked pasta and sprinkle with remaining pistachios.
- Serve immediately.
- Serves 2-4.

Sicilian Pasta

1 lb Shreiner's Smoked Bratwurst

2 medium onions, thinly sliced

1 clove Rhee's Garlic, minced

1 tbsp olive oil

2 medium zucchini, thinly sliced

½ tsp dried basil

¼ tsp dried oregano

¼ tsp salt

dash black pepper

2 large tomatoes, seeded and cut into
large pieces

hot cooked Ladson's Spaghetti

grated Parmesan cheese (optional)

- Break sausage into pieces and cook in large skillet until lightly browned; drain and set aside.
- Place onions, garlic and oil in same skillet.
- Sauté and stir over medium heat until onions are soft and lightly browned.
- Add zucchini, basil, oregano, salt and pepper; cook 5 minutes.
- Add tomatoes; cover and simmer 10 minutes, stirring occasionally.
- Serve over spaghetti with Parmesan cheese.
- Serves 4-5.

Fettuccine with Ham, Zucchini and Sweet Peppers

1 lb Beck's Mesquite Ham, cut into
6¼" slices

1 tbsp olive oil

2 small zucchini, sliced

1 red, yellow or green bell pepper, cut
into 2¼" x 3¼" strips

1 tsp crushed dried oregano

1 clove garlic, minced

12 oz fresh Ladson's Fettuccine

⅔ cup Shamrock® Half and Half

⅓ cup fresh basil leaves, cut into thin
pieces (optional)

⅓ cup sun dried tomatoes, blanched and
chopped (optional)

2 tbsp grated Parmesan cheese

freshly ground black pepper

basil to garnish

- Stack ham slices, cut lengthwise into ¼" strips; halve strips crosswise; set aside.
- In skillet, heat oil over medium high heat.
- Stir in next 4 ingredients; cook 5-6 minutes until zucchini is tender.
- Meanwhile, cook pasta according to pkg directions, add ham to pasta during last minute of cook time.
- Drain pasta; return to hot pan.
- Stir in zucchini mixture, cream, basil and tomatoes; toss thoroughly.
- Transfer to serving platter.
- Sprinkle with Parmesan cheese, season with pepper, garnish with basil.
- Serve immediately.
- Serves 5.

DISCOVERING THE COLORADO PLATEAU

"It can be approached only from the south and after entering it there is nothing to do but leave. Ours has been the first and will doubtless be the last party of whites to visit this profitless locality."
—Lieutenant Joseph Christmas Ives after hiking to the bottom of the Grand Canyon in 1858.

Well, Lieutenant, more than two million people now visit the Grand Canyon each year. Arizona historians frequently cite your short-sightedness. In fact, your report to Congress on all of western and northern Arizona indicated it didn't amount to much.

Given the values of 1858, and the problems of exploring the Colorado Plateau at that time, who can blame you? You were not looking for the scenic attractions that would make the plateau one of the favored destinations of American travelers. Still, some of your contemporaries were more optimistic about this part of Arizona.

Let's see, how can we organize a quick exploration of the jumbled wonders found on the Colorado Plateau? Arbitrary state boundary lines intersect at Four Corners, where Arizona meets Utah, Colorado and

New Mexico. Arizona's share of the Colorado Plateau extends southward and westward from Four Corners, rising to its southern limit at the Mogollon Escarpment, a jagged tear running northwest-to-southeast across the face of Arizona. Where it is most prominent, the escarpment is known as the Mogollon Rim, a 2,000-foot cliff.

The plateau is sliced deeply by the Colorado River gorge, which includes the Grand Canyon. Near the Utah border Glen Canyon Dam, completed in 1966, impounds Lake Powell, which extends far up into the canyons of Utah; the lake has 1,900 miles of shoreline, most of it vertical. Lake Powell was named for Major John Wesley Powell, the one-armed explorer who took wooden boats through the canyons in 1869 and again in 1872.

The starkly beautiful land north of the river is called the Arizona Strip and within the Strip is the Kaibab Plateau, an isolated island of forest. But for the arbitrary nature of boundary surveyors, the strip would be part of Utah, whose congressmen tried to claim it early in this century.

The Navajo Indian Reservation, largest in America, fills the region from Four Corners to a point 125 miles west, and about that far south. It is a land of mesa upon mesa, with an occasional lumpy mountain range. The Navajo Nation completely surrounds the much smaller Hopi reservation.

The Navajo Nation also takes in some of the prehistoric ruins mentioned in Chapter One: stunningly beautiful Canyon de Chelly and its tributary Canyon del Muerto, where members of several prehistoric cultures once grew food and fiber; the Anasazi ruins at Keet Seel and Betatikin in Navajo National Monument, where gully-cutting of precious farmland may have put an end to farming.

The natural wonders of the Colorado plateau first came to the attention of Americans in the 1850s, while the national government was plotting new roads to California. Captain Lorenzo Sitgreaves of the Army Corps of Topographical Engineers led the first expedition in 1851.

Sitgreaves had only a mule train to supply his party, and that wasn't enough. His soldiers, scientists and guides were in sorry shape by the time they reached California. Frequently the party had to camp while hunters were dispatched to find deer or antelope to feed the men. Subsequent expeditions would use wagons to carry supplies, and one even tried camels.

Yet Sitgreaves' observations became a litany as other explorers followed him: the fraudulence of rivers like the Puerco and the Little Colorado, which flowed only at certain times of the year; the potential for grazing cattle on the vast grasslands of the region's high plains; the beautiful, volcanic San Francisco Peaks standing like a beacon for travelers, almost dead center of northern Arizona. The tallest peak, Humphreys, is the tallest in Arizona, rising to 12,643 feet.

Sitgreaves also found, and wondered at, the ruins of Wupatki mentioned earlier: "They are evidently the ruins of a large town, as they occurred at intervals for an extent of eight or nine miles, and the ground was thickly strewed with fragments of pottery in all directions."

Right. Anthropologists now know that the Sinagua people farmed south of the Wupatki site until the winter of 1064 and 1065, when the volcano now known as Sunset Crater erupted. Survivors of the eruption moved northward, and soon found that volcanic ash made the ground more fertile for growing the grains, squash and beans on which they subsisted.

Members of other cultures joined the Sinagua in the scattered villages that now make up Wupatki National Monument. There is evidence that Hohokam traders from the south brought in artifacts from Mexico. Then drought drove the Sinagua south to other communities; yet another drought ended their civilization.

Lieutenant Amiel W. Whipple, the next explorer after Sitgreaves, carried ample supplies on both his expeditions. The first, beginning in the fall of 1853, also celebrated the region's first "company" or "office" Christmas party.

Whipple had about one hundred men in his party, including Mexican teamsters and herders to keep his wagon train and his livestock supply rolling. But by December 24, as the expedition traveled up a long, forested slope toward the base of the San Francisco Peaks, the problems of traveling through light snow sapped the party. Whipple declared two days of rest.

Whipple wrote, "Several of the party went out to hunt turkeys and other game, thinking to have a feast, but were quite unsuccessful. One young hunter got on the trail of a bear, but the footprints were so enormous that he preferred to return to camp."

Whipple ordered double rations for everyone. And the officers scrounged up some wine and eggs with which to make eggnog (plus some canned oysters for the officers' mess). A Lieutenant Jones invited everyone to bring his tin cup to Jones' tent for a drink.

H.B. Mollhausen, a naturalist and draftsman who wrote a delightful account of the trip, recorded: "No one had a previous engagement, nor was it at all tempting to decline, and as soon as the night set in and the stars began to flitter in the deep blue firmament and to look down upon us between the snowy branches, the company began to assemble at the appointed spot."

Speeches were made, toasts offered, songs sung, guns fired in the air. Then the Mexican teamsters and herders gave new meaning to the term "lighting" the tree: they set a grove of pines on fire for a grand and hazardous finale.

So joyous was the party that not everyone wanted to think about food the following day. But John Sherbourne, an assistant scientist, wrote in his diary: "Visions of roast turkeys, plum puddings and mince pies are rolling through my brain. I would like a slice off one of the many New England puddings today...Still I would not have it thought we were destitute of all the luxuries of life. I will give you the 'Bill of Fare' of our mess at dinner. 'Leg of roast mutton,' 'Beef a la mode,' 'Bass,' 'Wild Duck,' 'roast squirrel,' and 'claret' formed part of the Bill."

Lieutenant Edward F. Beale, the man who earlier had carried news of the California gold rush to the East, explored the 35th parallel across Arizona in 1857, using camels as beasts of burden. This was part of a government camel experiement that ranged from Texas to California.

Beale liked the way camels could live off the land, while carrying dried corn to feed lesser beasts in his caravan.

"I look forward to the day when every mail route across the continent will be conducted and worked altogether with the economical and noble brute," Beale wrote. But the Civil War interrupted the experiment, and then railroads began to displace other means of carrying the mail.

As he reached the Colorado River, Beale traded with Mojave Indian farmers for provisions to carry his caravan to its final destination, Fort Tejon, California. He wrote, "In a day, we had secured a hundred bushels of corn and beans, pumpkins, watermelons, and cantaloupes."

Beale's mission was to establish a national wagon road to California. The route evolved into U.S. Route 66, the storied "Main Street of America," replaced by today's Interstate 40. The year after Beale's trek, Lieutenant Ives, who had taken a steamboat up the Colorado River to the area of today's Lake Mead, crossed the plateau from west to east, reversing the direction of most explorations.

All of the explorers helped lay the foundation for a railroad route to California along the 35th parallel. The Atlantic & Pacific (later the Santa Fe) built a railroad across northern Arizona between 1880 and 1883. The railroad opened up a prosperous lumbering industry in the forests that stretched away from the new sawmill town of Flagstaff, and fostered cattle ranching all across the plateau.

W.J. Murphy, who later would help build an irrigated farming empire in the Salt River Valley, hopscotched across northern Arizona as a grading contractor, preparing roadbed for the A&P. His wife Laura and three small children followed in the unsprung wagons that carried feed for Murphy's mules. Laura bought provisions where she could. In a letter to relatives in Illinois, she told of buying two sacks of flour for nine dollars at Flagstaff.

Later, she wrote of the Christmas dinner she prepared in the grading camp near Peach Springs in 1881: "We gave the men, thirty-three in number, a grand Christmas dinner: roast meats, potatoes, onions, tomatoes, two large milk pans full of pudding (made of a layer of steamed sweet cake, then a layer of cooked raisins and so on, filled in with a dressing made of water and vinegar thickened with corn starch and flavored with lemon with a thin consistency, a delightful dish), pies (made of apple and raisin flavored with lemon in imitation of mince pie), cheese, and gooseberry sauce . . . This sumptuous repast had the effect designed, that of making the men so comfortable that not any of them went to the saloon a mile away where we were afraid some would celebrate."

Two of the five Babbitt brothers of Cincinnati rode a train west to Flagstaff in 1886 and bought a ranch. Soon they sold their grocery store in Cincinnati and all five brothers were in Flagstaff. Seeing the money to be made selling provisions, both those delivered by rail and from local truck gardens and bean farms, they founded a mercantile empire that survives today. One of their descendants, former Arizona Governor Bruce Babbitt, pursued the Democratic presidential nomination in 1988.

The Santa Fe created a string of railroad towns across northern Arizona—Winslow, Williams, Ash Fork, Seligman, Kingman—and each had a "Harvey House," one of the hotels and dining rooms of the Fred Harvey Company. "Harvey girls" recruited to staff the dining rooms became a part of American lore. They were handsome women, in the context of the frontier, and good candidates for wives.

The Grand Canyon was at first exploited by miners, who took up the tourist trade as a lucrative sideline; the Canyon was not protected as a national park until 1919. The Grand Canyon Railway, ultimately a branch of the Santa Fe, began in 1901 to carry passengers from the mainline at Williams. The railroad and Fred Harvey diligently promoted tourism at the Canyon, before automobiles began carrying waves of American travelers west along Route 66. In an odd turnabout, the Grand Canyon Railway, closed since the 1960s, was revived in 1989 as a tourist railroad. One of its goals was to reduce the number of automobiles crowding Grand Canyon Village.

Apparently not all of the Harvey girls were gracious and pliant. An engineer for the Grand Canyon Railway asked in Williams one morning about 1905 for a larger plate for his pancakes; he liked lots of syrup on them. The waitress refused. He could get by with the customary plate, she said. So the engineer spread his pancakes on the counter and drowned them in syrup.

One of the bravest migrations into Arizona occurred in the 1870s and 1880s, when the Church of Jesus Christ of Latter-day Saints sent Mormon colonists from Utah trekking across the plateau to spread the influence of the church. Two sons of the Latter-day Saints' President Brigham Young established a ranch and a small fort near Flagstaff. Other Mormon colonizers spread all across the plateau, and fanned out into the valleys of central Arizona, mainly the valleys of the Gila and Salt Rivers.

On the Colorado Plateau, the Mormons built towns along the Little Colorado River and in the area of the White Mountains, where the river begins. They built small irrigation dams on the river and its tributaries.

The well-worn trail between Utah and Arizona became known as the Honeymoon Trail. Latter-day Saints beliefs require that the faithful be married in a Latter-day Saints temple, and Arizona colonizers had to travel to the temple at St. George, Utah, until the Arizona Temple opened at Mesa in 1927. So large parties of Mormon lovers and their families trekked back and forth in trains of wagons during the late nineteenth and early twentieth centuries.

Mormons are characterized by thrift, industry, and large families. Their farms, ranches and grist mills helped feed the people and livestock moving into the region. The Plateau never experienced the population booms that occurred elsewhere in Arizona, because it had neither mineral wealth nor large irrigation projects.

Another Mormon trait is a sense of humor. Each Groundhog Day, residents of the predominantly Latter-day Saints town of Snowflake gather for a breakfast of ground hog—sausage to you. The community's name, by the way, has nothing to do with the weather. It is compounded of the names of two pioneers, Erastus Snow and William J. Flake.

Others will disagree, but when someone says "Arizona cuisine" I always think of the family reunions and potluck dinners of the White

Mountains region. They include salads and casseroles that combine the flavors of northern Europe with those of Mexico, and there's a strong element of whatever is available from the garden. You'll find green chili in many of these dishes, while red chili con carne is used as a side dish or a condiment.

In the autumn of 1881, Alfred and Ruth Randall and five children were sent by the Latter-day Saints church to settle what would become the village of Pine, Arizona. At the top of the Mogollon Rim, just above Pine, Alfred stopped to tie large logs to the rear of his wagons. That would help slow their descent down the face of the 2,000-foot-tall Rim, and keep them from running over the horses. Ruth and the children would walk.

Ruth, expecting another child, sat on a stump and began to cry. A 10-year-old son asked, "What's the matter, Ma?"

"Son, it just looks like your father is dragging us down to hell."

Family histories recall that Ruth, like other trail-weary Mormon wives, came to love her new home in the Tonto Basin below the Rim. So did many other people.

Let an earlier visitor, Captain John G. Bourke describe the region as he first saw it in 1871: "[The Mogollon Rim] is a strange upheaval, a strange freak of nature, a mountain canted up one one side; one rides along the edge and looks down two and three thousand feet into what is termed the 'Tonto Basin,' a weird scene of grandeur and rugged beauty. The 'Basin' is a basin only in the sense that it is all lower than the ranges enclosing it . . . but its whole triangular area is so cut up by ravines, arroyos, small stream beds and hills of very good height, that it may safely be pronounced one of the roughest places on the globe."

The Rim and the Basin have combined to become one of the favorite summer retreats of those who live in Arizona's desert cities. Several tiny creeks begin under the Rim and flow southward, growing to young rivers as they enter the systems of the Verde and Salt rivers.

The basin's central town is Payson, which was an isolated village until after World War II. Lewis R. Pyle, a pioneer whom I knew when I was a kid, used to have to haul Payson's groceries in from Phoenix or Flagstaff on burro pack trains. Picturesque Pine and colorful Strawberry might be called suburbs of Payson, although there are now summerhome subidivisions which may surpass them in population.

Western novelist Zane Grey was one of the regular visitors in the area. He kept a comfortable hunting lodge in the basin during the 1920s (it was destroyed by a 1990 forest fire) and some of his novels were set in Arizona.

One of his novels, *To The Last Man*, was based on the Pleasant Valley War of the 1880s, one of the bloodiest chapters in Arizona history. The war, essentially a ranchers' feud which killed at least thirty men, was centered a few miles southeast of Payson, but it raged over a much larger region.

West of the basin, the Verde River gives life to the broad, scenic Verde Valley; then the river plunges into a series of narrow canyons en route to Phoenix. Two of the prettier panoramic views in Arizona are from Interstate 17, where it enters the Verde Valley from the north and from the south.

The valley's farms originally supplied soldiers and miners in the 1860s and 1870s. It was from the historic Army post at Camp Verde, now a state historic park, that General George Crook launched a decisive campaign against Apaches in the mid-1870s. Now many of the farms along the Verde have been subdivided into retirement acreages.

Farther west are the Bradshaw Mountains and the town of Prescott, once a territorial capital and now a favored retreat from the big city. During the years it was capital (from 1864 to 1867 and again from 1877 to 1889), Prescott grew in the manner of a New England or midwestern town. Its courthouse square, and streets of fine Victorian homes, have been faithfully preserved. The pine forest which surrounds Prescott was one of the earliest summer home refuges for Phoenix residents who needed to escape summer heat before mechanical cooling was invented. The town's wealthier residents got together about 1900 and began building their own enclave at Iron Springs, and other summer camps and resort areas followed.

Technically, these last three areas—the Tonto Basin, the Verde Valley, the Bradshaws—are not part of the Colorado Plateau. Rather, they form a transition zone between plateau and desert.

Yet in the minds of those who live in the desert metropolis formed by Phoenix and its suburbs, these areas still mean escape and renewal in Arizona's high country.

The last several generations have come increasingly to value the land not for the wealth it can produce (although scenery creates quite a lot of wealth in Arizona), but simply because it's there.

I'm not sure Lieutenant Ives would understand that. But then, you have to give an explorer a lot of latitude.

VEGETABLES

Arizona's rugged beauty

South of the Border Zucchini

3-4 medium zucchini	• Slice zucchini into thick slices.
1 tsp olive oil	• Sauté in oil; add salsa.
½ cup Desert Rose Red Salsa	• Simmer 10 minutes; add cheese. Stir
2 cups shredded Cheddar or American cheese	on low heat until cheese melts.
	• Serves 4-6.

Evergreen Zucchini

3 lbs Young's Farm Zucchini, cut in ½" slices	• In covered skillet, cook zucchini with salt in water until just tender, 8-10 minutes; drain.
1 tbsp salt	
1½ cups water	• Add remaining ingredients; heat, stirring occasionally.
1 cup chopped parsley	
¼ cup butter, softened	• Serves 10-12.
2 tbsp instant minced onion	
1 Sunkist® Lemon to yield: ½ tsp fresh grated lemon peel and 2 tbsp fresh squeezed lemon juice	

Spaghetti Squash with Salsa

1 medium spaghetti squash	• Cut squash in half; scoop out seeds.
2 tbsp butter	• Top with butter, bake at 350 degrees 1 hour.
½ cup Desert Rose Red Salsa	
½ cup canned tomato sauce	• When flesh shreds easily, scrape out with fork; place in saucepan with remaining ingredients.
½ cup grated Parmesan or Romano cheese	
	• Heat, stirring, until warm.
	• Serves 2-4.

Stuffed Zucchini

3 medium zucchini, unpeeled
1 tbsp salt
1½ cups water
2 tbsp butter
½ cup chopped fresh mushrooms
2 tbsp all-purpose flour
½ tsp salt
¼ tsp Santa Cruz Chili &
Spice Oregano
1 cup shredded Monterey Jack cheese
2 tbsp Foremost® Sour Cream
¼ cup grated Parmesan cheese

- Cook whole zucchini in boiling salted water, covered, 10-12 minutes. Drain; cut in half lengthwise.
- Scoop out centers, leaving ¼" thick shell; chop pulp.
- In a skillet, melt butter; sauté mushrooms. Stir in flour, salt and oregano; remove from heat.
- Stir in Monterey Jack cheese, sour cream and zucchini pulp.
- Fill shells, using ¼ cup filling for each. Top with Parmesan cheese.
- Broil until hot and bubbly, 3-5 minutes.
- Serves 3-6.

Eggplant-Zucchini Supreme

2 medium Copperhead Onions, sliced
1 clove garlic, minced
4 tbsp olive oil
2 medium tomatoes, diced
1 large green pepper, cut into ½" strips
1 large red pepper, cut into ½" strips
1 unpared small eggplant, diced
2 small zucchini, cut into ½" slices
½ cup sliced mushrooms
2 bay leaves
¼ cup crisp bacon bits
2 tsp salt
⅛ tsp pepper
½ cup Malcolm's Honey

- Sauté onions with garlic in Dutch oven in hot oil until tender.
- Add tomatoes, peppers, eggplant, zucchini, mushrooms and bay leaf. Sauté over medium heat, stirring occasionally, 15-20 minutes.
- Add bacon bits, salt and pepper to vegetables; cover, simmer 15 minutes.
- Uncover, simmer 10 minutes; remove bay leaf.
- Add honey; stir thoroughly.
- Serve immediately.
- Serves 4-6.

Eggplant Parmesan

2-3 small eggplants cut in ½" slices
salt
⅓ cup all-purpose flour
¼ cup butter
1 (15 oz) can tomato sauce
1 tsp Sahuaro Spice Co. Basil
1½ cups shredded UDA Seal of Arizona Mozzarella Cheese
½ cup grated Parmesan cheese

- Preheat oven to 350 degrees.
- Sprinkle both sides of eggplant slices lightly with salt; spread in 1 layer on platter or board.
- After 20 minutes, pat eggplant dry with paper towels.
- Dip each slice in flour; shake off excess.
- Heat butter over low to medium heat in heavy 12" skillet. Brown eggplant slices, a few at a time; transfer to paper towels.
- Combine tomato sauce and basil. Pour ½ cup tomato sauce into buttered 1½ qt shallow baking dish.
- Spread layer of eggplant slices over sauce. Sprinkle on layer of mozzarella and Parmesan cheeses.
- Add remainder of eggplant slices, tomato sauce, mozzarella and Parmesan cheeses. Cover with foil.
- Bake 20 minutes. Uncover; bake 5 minutes.
- Serves 4.

Grilled Green Onions

2 tbsp vegetable oil
15 green onions, washed and trimmed
2 tbsp Sonoran Seasoning
½ cup Prickly Pear Barbecue Glaze

- Brush oil liberally over green onions; sprinkle with seasoning.
- Grill over hot coals 2-3 minutes, turning frequently until crispy and lightly browned.
- Brush glaze on green onions or serve glaze as dipping sauce.
- Serves 4-5.

Cheesy Onions

1½ lbs small Young's Farm Onions
4 slices Beck's Bacon, cooked and crumbled
3 tbsp butter
3 tbsp all-purpose flour
½ tsp salt
½ tsp Worcestershire sauce
⅛ tsp pepper
1 cup milk
1 cup shredded Cheddar cheese
¼ cup grated Parmesan cheese

- Peel onions; leave whole. Parboil onions in enough water to cover until fork tender, 20-25 minutes; drain.
- Arrange onions in buttered shallow baking dish. Sprinkle bacon over onions.
- Melt butter in medium saucepan.
- Stir in flour, salt, Worcestershire sauce and pepper until smooth.
- Remove from heat; gradually stir in milk.
- Bring to boil, stirring constantly. Boil and stir 1 minute.
- Stir in Cheddar cheese until melted.
- Pour sauce over onions and bacon; sprinkle with Parmesan cheese.
- Broil 4"-6" from heat source until mixture is hot and bubbly and cheese is golden, about 4 minutes.
- Serve immediately.
- Serves 4.

Spinach N' Cheese Casserole

2 (10 oz) pkgs frozen chopped spinach
2 Hickman's Eggs
2 tbsp all-purpose flour
1 tsp caraway seeds
½ tsp onion salt
⅛ tsp pepper
1 cup Carnation® Cottage Cheese
⅓ cup shredded, processed American cheese

- Cook spinach according to pkg directions; drain well.
- Beat eggs and flour with rotary beater until smooth; stir in caraway seeds, onion salt, pepper and cottage cheese. Fold into spinach.
- Spoon into 1 qt casserole; top with grated cheese.
- Bake in 350 degree oven 20 minutes.
- Serves 6-8.

Green Beans with Mustard Sauce

2 lbs fresh green or wax beans
3 tbsp butter
3 tsp Arizona Champagne Mustard Sauce
½ tsp salt
¼ tsp Sahuaro Spice Co. White Pepper
4 tbsp wheat germ

- Trim and cut green or wax beans into 2″ pieces.
- Steam 7 minutes; remove from heat and keep warm.
- Melt butter in small saucepan; stir in mustard, salt and pepper. Stir over low heat 2 minutes.
- Drain beans, pour mustard sauce and wheat germ over beans; toss gently.
- Serves 8.

Green Pea Casserole

⅓ cup chopped Young's Farm Onion
⅓ cup chopped green pepper
⅓ cup chopped celery
1½ tsp Shamrock® Margarine
1 (8 oz) pkg frozen peas, cooked
1 (10.75 oz) can cream of mushroom soup
¼ cup Shamrock® Milk
1 (2 oz.) jar chopped pimentos
1 (10.75 oz) can water chestnuts, drained and sliced
bread crumbs to top

- Sauté onion, green pepper and celery in margarine until tender.
- Cook peas according to pkg directions; drain.
- Mix soup and milk; combine with remaining ingredients.
- Pour into 1¼ qt casserole.
- Cover, put in refrigerator overnight.
- When ready to serve, sprinkle with crumbs.
- Bake in preheated oven at 350 degrees 25-30 minutes.
- Serves 6-8.

Hacienda Frijoles

1 (2 lb) pkg pinto beans
water
2 tsp salt
2 large onions, chopped
2 cloves garlic, minced
1 (16 oz) can chopped tomatoes
1 cup Desert Rose Barbacoa Sauce or Enchilada Sauce
1 (4 oz) can chopped green chilies, drained
1/4 tsp cumin
1/2 tsp pepper

- Rinse beans under cold running water.
- Place in large kettle and cover with cold water 2" above beans. Add salt; bring to boil.
- Lower heat and simmer, covered, 1 hour.
- Stir in onions, garlic, tomatoes, sauce, green chilies, cumin and pepper until well blended; return to boil.
- Lower heat and simmer until beans are tender, about 1 hour.
- Serves 8.

Gourmet Macaroni and Cheese

1 (7 oz) pkg Creamettes® Elbow Macaroni
3 tbsp Shamrock® Butter
3 tbsp all-purpose flour
1/2 tsp salt
1/4 tsp oregano
dash pepper
1 2/3 cups Shamrock® Milk
1/2 cup sliced onion rings, separated
1 1/2 cups shredded Cheddar cheese
1/4-1/3 cup crumbled bleu cheese

- Preheat oven to 350 degrees.
- Prepare macaroni according to pkg directions; drain.
- Melt butter in medium saucepan.
- Blend in flour, salt, oregano and pepper until smooth.
- Remove from heat; gradually stir in milk. Bring to boil, stirring constantly.
- Boil and stir 1 minute; remove from heat.
- Spread half of macaroni in buttered 2 qt rectangular baking dish; top with half of onion rings.
- Sprinkle half of cheeses over onion rings.
- Pour half of cream sauce over all; repeat.
- Bake 25-30 minutes.
- Serve immediately.
- Serves 5-6.

Chutnied Rice

4 tbsp butter, divided
½ cup slivered almonds
1 onion, minced
½ cup chopped celery
1 cup rice
2 cups chicken stock
½ cup Sallie's Apricot Cherry Chutney
¼ cup minced Fresh Touch Gardens Parsley
slivered almonds to garnish

- Melt 2 tbsp butter in heavy pan; add almonds.
- Sauté over high heat until light brown; remove and reserve.
- Melt remaining butter in pan, sauté onions and celery 5 minutes.
- Add rice, stirring well to evenly coat.
- Add stock and chutney; bring to boil; cover, reduce heat, simmer 15-20 minutes.
- Serve sprinkled with parsley and almonds.
- Serves 4.

Zesty Rice

2 cups cooked white or brown rice
½ cup Desert Rose Red Salsa
½ cup grated Cheddar cheese
¼ cup sliced black olives

- Combine cooked rice with salsa; top with cheese.
- Sprinkle olives on top of cheese; bake uncovered 20 minutes at 350 degrees.
- Serves 4-6.

Jamaican Dirty Rice

1 (14 oz) can coconut milk
1 (15 oz) can red kidney beans, with liquid
½ tsp dried thyme
2 Fresh Touch Gardens Green Onions, minced
1 Fresh Touch Gardens Jalapeno, seeded and minced
2 cloves garlic, minced
¼ tsp black pepper
pinch salt
1 cup basmati rice

- Measure coconut milk.
- Add bean liquid to make 2 cups total.
- Bring to boil with beans; add thyme, onions, jalapeno, garlic, pepper and salt.
- Reduce heat; simmer 5 minutes.
- Add rice; bring to boil, reduce heat, cover and simmer undistrubed until done, 25-30 minutes. This rice will be more sticky than regular white rice.
- Serves 6.

Baked Potato Wedges

4 large unpeeled potatoes
1 tbsp grated Parmesan cheese
1 tbsp paprika
¼ cup vegetable oil
1 tsp salt
½ tsp pepper
½ tsp Sahuaro Spice Co. Garlic Powder

- Wash potatoes, cut in wedges.
- Place skin down in baking dish.
- Mix remaining ingredients; brush on potatoes.
- Bake at 350-375 degrees 1 hour.
- Leftovers can be reheated or fried.
- Serves 6-8.

Boiled New Potatoes with Vinaigrette Dressing

¼ cup virgin olive oil
1 clove garlic, finely minced
2 tbsp white wine vinegar
1 tbsp Arizona Champagne Mustard Sauce
½ tsp black pepper
3 tbsp Arizona Herbal Spice Dip Mix
2¼ lbs new potatoes, sliced and cooked

- In small skillet, heat oil; sauté garlic. Do not brown.
- Pour into bowl; let cool. Add vinegar, mustard sauce, pepper and dip mix.
- Pour dressing over potatoes.
- Serves 5-6.

Refried Beans
—Recipe of United Presbyterian Women
Submitted by Colorado River Indian Tribe

3 lbs pinto beans
1 lb slab bacon
2 tbsp salt
½ cup shortening
grated cheese

- Put beans into large pot; cover with boiling water.
- Cut bacon into 2″ squares; add to beans.
- Add salt, cover and cook 3 hours. Add water as necessary to keep from scorching.
- Place shortening in large skillet; heat until grease smells scorched.
- Put drained beans in skillet and mash fine; fry lightly.
- Garnish with grated cheese and serve hot.
- Serves 12-16.

Potatoes Norma Ole!

2 tbsp Authentic Cowboy Chili Seasoning

3 tbsp melted butter

3 large potatoes, peeled and cut into slices

1 (7 oz) can diced green chilies

½ cup grated Cowboy Cheese

- Combine chili seasoning with melted butter in bowl. Set aside 5 minutes.
- Add potatoes; mix thoroughly.
- Fry in skillet until desired degree of doneness. Add diced green chilies, mix thoroughly, stir just long enough for chilies to be warmed.
- Sprinkle with grated Cowboy cheese.
- Serve immediately.
- Serves 8.

Potato Lasagne

4-5 medium potatoes, sliced

2 lbs ground Arizona Beef

1 Copperhead Onion, chopped

1 (10.75 oz) can Cheddar cheese soup

oregano

1 (15 oz) can tomato sauce

1 cup shredded mozzarella cheese

- Line 9" x 13" cake pan with 2 layers of potatoes.
- Sauté hamburger with onion until brown; drain and add soup.
- Pour over potatoes.
- Spread tomato sauce over mixture, sprinkle with oregano; cover with foil.
- Bake 1-1¼ hours or until done.
- Sprinkle cheese over mixture the last 5 minutes of baking.
- Serves 6-8.

IRRIGATED EMPIRES

"Life blood of valley turned into its arteries by Theodore Roosevelt: Triumphant ending of the Great Project."
—Headline in *The Arizona Republican* after Roosevelt Dam was dedicated March 18, 1911.

A few months before Roosevelt Dam was dedicated, winning San Francisco horse breeder C.A. Durfee came to Phoenix to race some of his horses at the Territorial Fair. A reporter heard Durfee had freighted through the area back in the 1860s, and asked him what Phoenix was like then.

Durfee said, "In 1863, when I camped here, there wasn't any town at all." Then Durfee saved the reporter's day with this story:

He had been working as a teamster, hauling grain from Sacaton, the largest of the Pima villages, to the mines at Wickenburg. He decided to quit, and asked his employer for $140 in back wages.

The freighter refused to pay him; if he did, the boss said, Durfee would move on, and he didn't want to lose such a good driver. Durfee quit anyway, and the driver who succeeded him was killed by Indians just outside Wickenburg.

Where Durfee had seen only creosote desert and mesquite flats before, in 1910 he found a lively little city of 11,000 people, up to its ears in civic awareness. There were demands for paved streets, new sewer lines, a new water system. A motorcycle policeman had been hired to make sure the town's 400 automobiles did not exceed the twelve miles per hour speed limit.

Phoenix was at the center of a growing agricultural empire. The best was yet to come, for Roosevelt Dam, nearing completion northeast of Phoenix, would give farmers a far more reliable supply of water and electricity.

What happened in the intervening years between 1863 and 1910? At the time Durfee was freighting through the area, former soldier John Smith was growing hay on the banks of Salt River. And adventuresome Jack Swilling, passing through the area, had seen the potential for irrigated farming.

Swilling had a farm at Wickenburg where he grew provisions for the new town and for the nearby Vulture Mine. Swilling organized the Swilling Irrigating and Canal Company, admitting friends to "shares" in the water to be taken from the Salt River; they would earn their shares by work, and farm the lands watered by their new canal.

In places, the ditch builders dug out old Hohokam canals that had been abandoned centuries earlier. The Swilling Ditch opened in 1868. By July of that year, a newspaper in Prescott reported that wheat and barley from the Salt River Valley were selling at Wickenburg for eight cents a pound, and a corn crop was coming along nicely.

Swilling called his new settlement "Phoenix" for the mythical bird of several ancient cultures which rose periodically from its own ashes. When a Phoenix townsite was established in 1870 west of Swilling's original settlement, the name Phoenix was applied by Brian Darrel Duppa, an English adventurer and a member of Swilling's original ditch company.

Other ditch companies followed, and larger canals were built. John

Smith, who had first grown hay nearby, thought his name sounded like an alias, so he went to court and had his name expanded to John Y.T. Smith; legend says the initials stood for "Yours Truly." He opened a store in Phoenix at a time when his dry goods still had to be shipped by boat from San Francisco to the Colorado River, then overland to Phoenix in wagons. Smith later opened the town's second flour mill.

Satellite towns grew up in the Salt River Valley. Mormons settled at Mesa and Lehi, east of Phoenix. Within a century, Mesa would absorb Lehi and become Arizona's third largest city. The town of Tempe grew at a place called Hayden's Ferry, east of Phoenix and on the south side of the Salt. It is now the home of Arizona State University, the territorial normal school that became a football powerhouse and one of the larger universities in the nation.

Northwest of Phoenix, a Dunkard temperance community was established at Glendale. Farmers from Illinois and Wisconsin founded towns named Peoria and Marinette. These three townsites were laid out by W.J. Murphy, the railroad contractor of Chapter Seven. In 1886 Murphy finished building the Arizona Canal forty-four miles across the north side of the Valley, carrying water from the Verde River.

Farmers began growing vegetables, fruit and cotton. Cotton, which had been grown by the Hohokam centuries before, would become Arizona's biggest cash crop. An enormous citrus industry was started. Murphy and other promoters lured a variety of people to the Salt River Valley. Some were investors who simply put up their money and returned to their homes in the East and Midwest. Then there were wealthy gentlemen farmers who created vast irrigated estates, such as William Henry Bartlett's showplace Sahuaro Ranch near Glendale. The ranch was a model fruit-growing operation, and is today a Glendale city park and museum, celebrating part of Arizona history too often overshadowed by stories of gunfighters and lost gold mines.

Many newcomers were farmers of more modest means, looking for a quarter-section on which to grow crops and a family. Developers and chambers of commerce conducted recruitment campaigns in California and the Midwest. Both the Southern Pacific and the Santa Fe railroads offered special one-way "colonist fares" to Arizona. (While both of Arizona's transcontinental railroads missed Phoenix, branch lines connected to the SP in 1886 and to the Santa Fe in 1895. That gave farmers competitive rates for shipping their products out to market.)

My old friend Herb Young, who lived to be 100, wrote a little book that explained some of the mysteries of surviving in Arizona Territory in the 1890s. His father homesteaded a farm and ranch west of Phoenix, at the very end of one of the irrigation canals.

Herb told of supplementing vegetables from the garden with quail, rabbits, doves and an occasional duck that landed on the stock pond.

"Pork was an occasional treat, but as in all cattle country, beef was king. Father would butcher a young steer, and then we would enjoy cuts that no one bothered to classify, but now would be called T-bone or porterhouse or club or filet mignon, and such common stuff as round steaks and rump roasts. Then, too, there were the soups and stews and chunky gravy.

"The remaining meat was cured to make jerky. To accomplish this, the lean meat was cut into strips, the fat cut away, and the strips salted and hung on wires in the sun. If the weather was hot, it took only a day or two for the meat to dry so hard it cracked. Then it was packed in cheesecloth sacks and stored, to be used when fresh meat was not at hand."

Occasionally, Herb's father bought a one hundred-pound block of ice at a factory in Phoenix, wrapped it in blankets and carried in home in a wagon. Ice was a luxury available in few areas of Arizona.

But Herb also explained the workings of the "cooler" used when ice was not available: "This box was made of lumber and was about four feet square and five feet tall, with legs that held it a foot above the ground. The legs were placed in tomato cans filled with water to keep out the house ants. The box was a frame covered by two thicknesses of gunny sacking. Two oil cans were placed on top. Each had a row of small holes poked along the lower edge on one side. When the cans were filled with water, the water trickled down over the sacking, keeping it moist. Evaporation kept the interior nice and cool."

An odd form of ranching took place in the Salt River Valley. Thousands of ostriches were grown here for their plumes, favored for women's hats and boas. One eastern visitor who sampled the drumstick of a young bird in 1906 declared it as good as chicken. The bird was rarely used for food, however, since a young one sold for $100 and a mature one for $1,000.

World War I, and changing fashion, killed the demand for plumes. Late in 1914, thousands of birds were being offered for $10 each. Now, each February, the town of Chandler southeast of Phoenix holds a popular ostrich festival, drawing thousands of fun-seekers.

The territorial capital had bounced from Prescott to Tucson and back to Prescott. When emerging Phoenix captured the seat of government in 1889, a Prescott editor accused Phoenix of wanting "the earth and the balance of the universe." Phoenix never denied it, not even to this day.

Yet farmers and townspeople were still at the mercy of the mercurial Salt River. In summer, it almost dried up, just when irrigation water was needed most. At other times of year it flooded, ruining farmlands, dwellings, railroad bridges. All during the 1890s, farmers schemed ways to build a high dam fifty-five miles northeast of Phoenix, in a canyon where Tonto Creek joined the Salt.

Financing was a major problem, however, and a committee was formed to find a solution. The committee was in place in 1902, when President Theodore Roosevelt signed the National Reclamation Act, allowing the Interior Department to build water storage dams with interest-free loans.

The Salt River Valley Water Users' Association was formed and Theodore Roosevelt Dam was begun at the Tonto Creek site. The dam was dedicated March 18, 1911, keystone of the nation's first multi-purpose reclamation project. The valley's farmers could not only feed people and animals in the territory, but ship thousands of carloads of produce to the rest of the world. Other dams were built on the Salt and its tributary Verde River. These dams have provided a large recreation bonus for Arizonans. There are 140,000 watercraft registered in this desert state, mostly power boats but a good number of sailboats and sailboards as well.

Smaller irrigation districts on the periphery of the valley collected water from other watersheds: the Agua Fria, the Hassayampa. The Hassayampa, which enters the Gila southwest of Phoenix, has a special niche in Arizona lore. It is said that anyone who drinks of its waters will never again tell the truth. For several decades, every prospector, mine promoter, hustler and free-thinker in Arizona was labeled "a Hassayamper."

W.J. Murphy might have been called a Hassayamper, but not to his face. Although his company was overextended and went into receivership in 1896, he had an enormous impact on the valley.

Beside his Arizona Canal he built a lodge to entertain investors who came out from the Midwest. The place he called Ingleside included a golf course of oiled sand, maybe the first such course in Arizona. Murphy may not have realized that golfing in the winter sunshine would become a major lure to winter visitors.

In 1909 and 1910, W.J.'s son Ralph Murphy turned Ingleside into a winter resort, the first in the Phoenix area. Ingleside also included an exclusive subdivision which drew such luminaries as U.S. Vice President Thomas R. Marshall, the man who said, "What this country needs is a good five-cent cigar."

Ralph Murphy's son, Merwin Murphy, remembered in 1989 how he used to come home from college and renew himself on the excellent food at the Ingleside. Olives were a big crop in the valley; at least two local companies bottled olive oil.

"Sometimes olives were a glut on the market," Merwin Murphy said, "and the menu at the inn advertised 'olive-fed turkeys.'"

Other famous resorts soon followed: the Arizona Biltmore, Jokake Inn (now part of the ritzy modern Phoenician Resort).

Dwight B. Heard's legacy was at least as enduring as Murphy's. He was a successful Chicago hardware executive who came to Phoenix for his health in 1895. Heard, his wife Maie and her father, A.C. Bartlett, invested a lot of money in farms, ranches and subdivision. Dwight Heard traveled to Egypt to study irrigation, and was a staunch supporter of Roosevelt Dam. He was a real estate broker, a subdivider, a newspaper publisher, a philanthropist, a political powerhouse. He persuaded Phoenix to acquire South Mountain Park, the largest municipal park in America, paying the federal government one dollar an acre.

At the time Dwight Heard died in 1929, the Heard Museum was nearing completion. The prestigious museum is today an internationally recognized museum of anthropology and native peoples. When she was appointed to the U.S. Supreme Court in 1980, former Arizona ranch girl Sandra Day O'Connor had to give up her voluntary chairmanship of the museum board, where she had helped push the Heard into the forefront of American museums.

At the opposite end of the economic scale were members of minority groups. Hispanics worked mostly as farm hands. Blacks were domestics, laborers, service workers in the town's hotels and restaurants. However, one black, William P. Crump, became a successful produce broker, shipping the valley's fruits and vegetables out by the carload to distant markets.

Chinese occupied a block-square enclave in downtown Phoenix. They grew vegetables, operated opium dens and gambling halls, and ran restaurants. In 1910 both the American Kitchen and the French Kitchen were run by Chinese. The Chinese were the first ethnic group to prosper and assimilate themselves into the Anglo community of Phoenix. Outside the city, Japanese grew vegetables and flowers on relatively small farms.

Prosperity ruled the valley nine months of the year, but in the summer, heat brought business to a crawl. Those who could afford it left town for the California shore or the mountains of Arizona.

The evaporative principle that Herb Young described was eventually applied to cooling homes and businesses. Between 1936 and 1946, evaporative cooling revolutionized life on the desert.

And by that time, veterans of World War II had found a new mobility and were looking for a new way of life. Many of them had trained in Arizona during the war, and now they came back. Like other western cities, Phoenix was built for the automobile, and its single-family homes sprawled across the farmland and the desert, giving newcomers lots of elbow room.

The area had many prominent farmers, but John M. Jacobs may deserve a special place in the annals of American groceries. During and after World War II, he developed 2,800 acres north of Phoenix. He grew some grain and fed some cattle, but mostly he was a vegetable grower, with his own packing sheds.

Jacobs exploited a "hole in the market." Arizona could provide vegetables to eastern cities in winter. When President George Bush declared his personal distate for broccoli in the spring of 1990, friends of Jacobs remembered when they had jokingly dubbed him "Broccoli King of America." Broccoli had been known mostly in Italy and in the New York region prior to World War II. Jacobs planted several hundred acres of the vegetable, and put it on dinner tables in New York and Boston at Thanksgiving.

In 1957, Park Central Shopping Center opened where the Central Avenue dairy had been. It was the first of the big regional malls, and a harbinger of the new shape of cities.

Tiny Scottsdale, begun in the 1880s as a citrus farming development, became "The West's Most Western Town" and a glitzy hub of the winter resort industry. For a long time, Arizona winters had drawn prominent Americans. Architect Frank Lloyd Wright had established Taliesin West, the studio that is now a major winter tourist attraction. Publisher Henry Luce and wife Clare Boothe Luce, an ambassador, playwright and congresswoman, had a winter home here. Irving Berlin used to write songs at the Biltmore. Novelist Clarence Buddington Kelland moved to Arizona and became a wheelhorse in Republican politics.

A friend of mine said the other day, after we had both flown back into Phoenix after vacations in the East. "I think of Arizona as being a flat, desert city, but when you really look at it, you see all the mountains."

Sharp, distinct mountains rise from the desert floor: Camelback Mountain in the heart of the resort district; the towering South Mountains with their overlooks, trails and picnic ramadas guarding the city from the south; a dozen other mountains within the city and its suburbs.

When Roosevelt Dam was dedicated, a newspaper editorial predicted Phoenix could grow to a population of 50,000. Its population is now pushing one million; the total population of its metropolitan area is around two million.

It is a metropolis of museums, theaters, colleges, universities, huge regional shopping malls and pricey pockets of boutiques, notably in glitzy Scottsdale. The valley is a place of well-known golf courses, horseback trails, cowboy steakhouses and five-star restaurants. There is a strong Mexican and Native American flavor to many of the attractions.

Some of the older towns have grown together, and there are several new communities that didn't exist thirty years ago: Carefree, Sun City and Sun City West, Fountain Hills, Sun Lakes, among others.

A few miles southwest of Phoenix, the Salt River joins the Gila. James Ohio Pattie reported in 1826 that the tributary Salt carried much more water than the broad, flat Gila. In a way the Gila is the boundary of our irrigated empire, and in a way it is not.

Pimas were growing irrigated crops along the Gila in 1694, when Father Kino first visited them. White men have extended narrow bands of farming along the Gila in both directions: east to the areas of Safford, Thatcher and Duncan, and west in the river valleys approaching Yuma and the Colorado River.

South of the Gila, however, another large farming area supports the cities of Casa Grande, Eloy, Florence, Coolidge. By the way, Casa Grande Ruins National Monument, the old Hohokam structure, is located not at the modern town of Casa Grande, but near Coolidge.

Florence, settled a few months before the Phoenix area, has done a great job of preserving its territorial buildings. The oldest of three standing Pinal County courthouses, dating from the 1870s, is Ernest W. McFarland State Park. McFarland was Arizona governor, U.S. Senate majority leader, and state Supreme Court justice.

The large, funnel-shaped agricultural region below the Gila points south, its spout pinching out south of Tucson. Most of the farming in this area is supported by deep wells. It is expensive farming, made feasible in part by the seasonal "hole in the market."

Pumping groundwater costs a lot, and it was in this area that Arizona's mythical dehydrated water was first introduced.

This miraculous substance was no doubt made of water imported from the Hassayampa River. Being lighter than regular water, dehydrated water reduces pumping costs enormously, to say nothing of wear and tear on pumps.

Cattle raised on dehydrated water can simply be sliced up and sold to taverns and markets as jerky, eliminating messy processing.

DESSERTS

A downtown Tucson oasis near El Mercado

Quick and Easy Holiday Parfait

2 cups Carnation® Cottage Cheese

1½ cups Carnation® Homogenized Milk

1 (3.75 oz) pkg instant lemon pudding mix

⅓ cup chopped candied lemon peel

⅓ cup chopped candied orange peel

½ cup halved candied red cherries

½ cup halved candied green cherries

⅓ cup toasted, sliced almonds

1 cup Carnation® Whip Cream, whipped

- Beat cottage cheese 4 minutes at medium speed with electric mixer.
- Add milk and pudding mix. Beat 1 minute longer on low speed.
- Chill 1 hour, or until mixture mounds from a spoon.
- Combine lemon peel, orange peel, red cherries, green cherries and almonds in bowl; mix well.
- Alternate layers of cottage cheese mixture and candied fruit mixture in parfait glasses.
- Chill until ready to serve.
- Just before serving, garnish with whipped cream.
- Serves 4.

Honey Fruit Fondue

½ cup butter

1 cup Foremost® Whipping Cream

⅓ cup Mountain Top Honey

¼ cup pineapple-apricot preserves

1½ tbsp cornstarch

¼ cup fresh squeezed Sunkist® Orange Juice

fruit pieces, dried fruit, chunks of angel food or pound cake, marshmallows

- Place butter, cream, honey and preserves in saucepan over medium heat.
- Heat until butter is melted and mixture is bubbly, stirring constantly. Reduce heat to low.
- Blend cornstarch and orange juice. Add to cream mixture; cook, stirring constantly, until thickened.
- Serve over fruit, cake or marshmallows.
- Makes 2⅓ cups.

Prickly Pear Jelly Roll

4 tbsp margarine

4 Laid in Arizona Eggs

¾ cup sugar

1 tsp vanilla or lemon juice

¾ cup all-purpose flour

1 tsp baking powder

½ tsp salt

1 (10 oz) jar Desert Kettle Prickly Pear Jelly

¼ cup powdered sugar

Instant Whip Whipped Topping

- Heat oven to 400 degrees.
- Melt margarine in 15" x 10½" x 1" jelly roll pan in oven as it heats.
- Spread evenly in pan; remove when melted.
- Beat eggs until thick and lemon yellow.
- Add sugar 1 tbsp at a time, beating after each addition.
- Add vanilla or lemon juice.
- Sift together flour, baking powder and salt; fold into egg batter in 2 additions.
- Spread batter evenly in pan.
- Bake 15-18 minutes, until golden brown.
- Remove from oven; let stand in pan 5 minutes.
- Invert pan on powdered sugar-dusted paper towels.
- Let stand 1 minute, gradually lift pan, easing cake out carefully with spatula.
- Trim crisp edges.
- Roll lengthwise, unroll and spread with prickly pear jelly.
- Re-roll and dust with powdered sugar.
- Cut into 1½" slices.
- Top slices with whipped topping.
- Serves 6-8.

Tarte A L'Orange Ambrosia

2 tbsp sugar
1 tsp cornstarch
1 tsp freshly grated orange peel
1/4 cup freshly squeezed orange juice
1 tbsp curacao or other orange-flavored liqueur
3 Sunkist® Oranges, peeled, cut into half cartwheel slices and well drained
6 (3"-4") baked tart shells
2 tbsp Sallie's Seasoning Toasted Coconut

- To make glaze, combine sugar and cornstarch in small saucepan; stir in orange peel and juice.
- Cook over medium heat, stirring until slightly thickened; stir in liqueur.
- Arrange orange half cartwheel slices in tart shells; spoon glaze over orange slices.
- Sprinkle with coconut; chill.
- Serves 6.

Spiced Grapefruit Upside-Down Cake

1 Sunkist® Grapefruit
1/3 cup Foremost® Butter
1/2 cup packed brown sugar
18 walnut halves
1 (16 oz) pkg pound cake mix
2 Laid In Arizona Eggs
milk
1 tsp cinnamon
1/8 tsp cloves

Topping:
1 cup Foremost® Whipping Cream
2 tbsp powdered sugar
peel of 1/2 Sunkist® Grapefruit, grated

- Finely grate peel of 1 grapefruit; reserve. Peel and cut grapefruit into 6 cartwheel slices and drain well.
- Preheat oven to 325 degrees.
- Melt butter in 9" square baking pan.
- Remove pan from oven; sprinkle brown sugar evenly over melted butter.
- Arrange grapefruit slices and walnut halves over sugar.
- In large bowl, prepare pound cake mix with eggs and milk according to pkg directions, adding cinnamon and cloves. Stir in grapefruit peel.
- Pour batter over grapefruit.
- Bake 50-55 minutes, until toothpick inserted in center comes out clean.
- Run knife around inside of baking pan; invert onto serving platter.
- For topping, whip cream with powdered sugar; gently fold in grated peel.
- Serve cake warm or cool with topping.
- Serves 8-9.

Montezuma's Castle near Flagstaff

Arizona Jelly Cake

1½ cups sifted all-purpose flour
1 tsp baking powder
½ tsp baking soda
½ tsp Sahauro Spice Co. Cloves
1 tsp Sahauro Spice Co. Cinnamon
1 tsp Sahauro Spice Co. Nutmeg
6 tbsp butter
½ cup brown sugar
2 eggs
3 tbsp cultured sour cream or yogurt
1 (10 oz) jar Cheri's Prickly Pear Jelly or Pomegranate Jelly

- Preheat oven to 350 degrees.
- Grease 7" tube pan.
- Sift together flour, baking powder, baking soda, cloves, cinnamon and nutmeg.
- In bowl, cream together butter and brown sugar; add eggs and beat to blend.
- Beat in sour cream or yogurt.
- Stir flour mixture into butter mixture until barely blended.
- Stir in jelly.
- Pour batter into tube pan; bake 30 minutes, or until done.
- While still warm, glaze top of cake with additional jelly.
- Serves 10-12.

Mocha Fudge Pudding Cake

1¼ cups sugar, divided
1 cup all-purpose flour
2 tsp baking powder
¼ tsp salt
½ cup Carnation® Butter
1 (1 oz) square unsweetened baking chocolate
½ cup milk
1 tsp vanilla
½ cup firmly packed light brown sugar
¼ cup cocoa
1 cup hot, strong Espressions Coffee
Carnation® Ice Cream

- Combine ¾ cup sugar, flour, baking powder and salt in mixing bowl.
- Melt butter with chocolate in saucepan over low heat; add to dry ingredients with milk and vanilla.
- Beat until smooth; pour into 8" square pan.
- Combine ½ cup sugar, brown sugar and cocoa in small bowl; sprinkle evenly over batter.
- Pour coffee over top; do not stir.
- Bake at 350 degrees 40 minutes, or until center is almost set.
- Serve warm with ice cream.
- Serves 8-10.

Lemon Layer Cake

½ cup shortening
1 cup Flagstaff Honey
2 Laid In Arizona Eggs
2 cups sifted flour
¾ tsp baking soda
½ tsp salt
2 tbsp lemon juice
¼ cup milk

Lemon Cream Filling:
1 egg yolk
2 tbsp sugar
1 tbsp cornstarch
⅛ cup Flagstaff Honey
⅛ cup water
⅛ cup lemon juice
⅛ tsp grated lemon peel
½ tbsp butter

Honey Frosting:
¼ cup Flagstaff Honey
¾ cup sugar
1 egg white
3 tbsp lemon juice
dash salt
¼ tsp grated lemon peel

- Cream shortening with honey until fluffy.
- Add eggs 1 at a time, beating well after each addition.
- Sift together flour, baking soda and salt. Add lemon juice to milk.
- Combine sifted dry ingredients to creamed mixture alternately with lemon soured milk.
- Pour into 2 greased 8″ layer cake pans.
- Bake 20-30 minutes in 350 degree oven.
- When done, remove from oven; cool slightly, and remove from pans.
- For filling, beat egg yolk in top of double boiler.
- Combine sugar and cornstarch; mix into egg yolk and add remaining ingredients.
- Cook over boiling water until mixture thickens, about 15 minutes, stirring frequently; cool.
- Spread filling on bottom layer of cooled cake; top with second layer of cake.
- Combine all frosting ingredients, except lemon peel, in top of double boiler.
- Place over boiling water; beat 7 minutes, or until frosting thickens and holds its shape.
- Remove from heat; add grated lemon peel.
- Continue beating until thick enough to spread.
- Spread on top and sides of lemon layer cake.
- Serves 10-12.

Apple Pie

6 cups sliced Brown's Apples

1, 9" unbaked 2 crust shell

1½ cup Flagstaff Honey

1½ tbsp lemon juice

¼ cup cornstarch

2 tsp cinnamon

1 tsp apple pie spice

1½ tsp margarine

- Preheat oven to 425 degrees.
- Arrange apples in pastry shell.
- Mix together honey, lemon juice, cornstarch, spices and margarine. Pour over apples.
- Slit top crust of pastry shell; cover apple mixture, sealing top and bottom crusts.
- Bake 40-50 minutes, until apples are tender.
- Serves 6-8.

Cheese Crumble Apple Pie

1, 9" unbaked pie shell

Topping:

½ cup all-purpose flour

⅓ cup sugar

⅓ cup firmly packed light brown sugar

½ tsp cinnamon

5 tbsp UDA Seal of Arizona Butter

Filling:

5-6 peeled, thinly sliced Valley's Finest Granny Smith Apples

1 tbsp fresh lemon juice

1½ cups shredded UDA Seal of Arizona Cheddar Cheese

4 tsp all-purpose flour

¼ tsp nutmeg

- Preheat oven to 375 degrees.
- Make high rim on pie shell.
- For topping, combine flour with sugars and cinnamon. Cut in butter; set aside.
- For filling, toss together apples and lemon juice.
- Mix together cheese, flour and nutmeg; toss with apples.
- Arrange apples in pie shell.
- Sprinkle on topping.
- Bake 40-50 minutes.
- Serve warm.
- Serves 8-10.

Cheddar-Peach Deep Dish Dessert

1 (1 lb 14 oz) can sliced
freestone peaches
⅓ cup sugar
2 tbsp Sunkist® Lemon Juice
1⅓ cups all-purpose flour
¼ tsp salt
⅛ tsp red pepper
½ cup butter
1 cup shredded UDA Seal of Arizona
Cheddar Cheese
⅓ cup peach syrup
ground ginger
vanilla ice cream

- Preheat oven to 350 degrees.
- Drain peaches, reserving ⅓ cup peach syrup; arrange in bottom of shallow 4 cup baking dish.
- Sprinkle with sugar, then lemon juice.
- Combine flour, salt and pepper; cut in butter until mixture resembles coarse meal. Mix in cheese.
- Sprinkle peach syrup over mixture, 1 tbsp at a time, mixing lightly with fork.
- Gather up dough with fingers. Roll on lightly floured surface to ⅜″ thick.
- Cut in ½″ strips; make a latticed top over peaches.
- Sprinkle with ginger. Bake 40-45 minutes.
- Serve warm, topped with vanilla ice cream.
- Serves 6.

Pumpkin Pie

2 cups fresh pumpkin puree
or
1 (1 lb) can pumpkin
½ tsp ginger
½ tsp cinnamon
1 tsp salt
4 Hickman's Eggs, slightly beaten
1 cup Mountain Top Honey
1 cup evaporated milk
1, 10″ unbaked pie shell

- In large bowl, blend pumpkin, ginger, cinnamon and salt.
- Beat in eggs, honey and milk.
- Pour into pie shell.
- Bake in oven at 400 degrees, 45-55 minutes, or until knife inserted 1″ from edge of pie comes out clean.
- Filling will set as pie cools.
- Serves 8-10.

Banshee Pie

18 chocolate wafer cookies
½ cup melted Shamrock® Butter
20 large marshmallows
¼ cup Shamrock® Milk
1 cup Shamrock® Whipping Cream
¼ cup creame de banana
¼ cup white creme de cacao

- Finely crush cookies; blend with melted butter.
- Press mixture into 9″ pie pan, reserving ¼ cup for topping; chill.
- Melt marshmallows in milk; cool.
- Beat cream until stiff; blend in liqueurs.
- Fold in marshmallow mixture. Pour into shell; sprinkle top reserved crumbs.
- Refrigerate until solid.
- Serves 8-10.

Peach Dessert

1 cup Arizona Vineyards Workers Red Wine
½ cup brown sugar
½ tsp ground fresh coriander
½ tsp ginger
½ tsp cinnamon
3 cups sliced peaches

- Mix together all ingredients, except peaches.
- Pour wine mixture over peaches; marinate in refrigerator 30 minutes-1 hour.
- Serves 4.

Uptown Sourdough Biscuit Dessert

1 (12 oz) pkg Territorial Gourmet Prospector Sourdough Biscuit Mix
1 (8 oz) pkg cream cheese, softened
1 mango or kiwi, any exotic fruit
1 (10 oz) jar Cheri's Arizona Harvest Prickly Pear Jelly

- Make biscuits according to pkg directions.
- Split warm biscuits; spread lightly with cream cheese.
- Top with fruit slice.
- Heat jelly in microwave dish to liquify; drizzle over fruit-topped biscuit.
- Makes 1 doz.

TOO THICK TO SWIM, TOO THIN TO PLOW

"The Colorado was lower than any of the residents at Fort Yuma had ever before known it. It could scarcely fall any lower without going entirely through its own bottom. A more capricious river does not exist. . . As a navigable stream it possesses some advantages during the dry season; boats can seldom sink in it; and for the matter of channels it has an unusual variety. The main channel shifts so often that the most skillful pilot always knows where it is not to be found by pursuing the course of his last trip."

—J. Ross Browne, Harper's New Magazine, 1864.

Believe it or not, Browne said some nice things about this country, and we'll get to them soon. But his reputation depended on witty hyperbole, and his slashing descriptions of Arizona are based on kernels of truth.

Southwestern rivers—the Rio Grande, the Gila, the Colorado—set their own pace. The Colorado, boundary between Arizona and California, is as independent as some of the crusty retirees who frequently fish its marshes.

Old-timers tell about a resident of Yuma who returned from his first trip to New York. A friend asked him what he thought of the Hudson.

"Couldn't tell," he said. "It had water in it the whole time I was there."

In fact, the Colorado River has not ever gone dry. Not in the 1860s and 1870s, when steamboats carried supplies upstream to be freighted to Arizona's interior. And not in the 1990s, when seven dams are in place along Arizona's borders. The dams calm the river, and settle out a lot of its legendary mud. They provide recreation all up and down the river—boating, skiing, fishing, observing migrating bird life.

Then the dams send some water to Los Angeles, and some to the Imperial Valley, and some to Baja California, and some to the interior of Arizona, and there is still water in the Colorado when it reaches the Gulf of California.

It did get lost a time or two, however. In the winter of 1905 and 1906, it broke its west bank and flowed into California's Imperial Valley, forming the Salton Sea and drying up the river bed below the break. And they tell of an Arizona couple who awakened one day to find the Colorado had changed courses and now went around the other side of their house.

"Well, we live in California now," the husband said.

"Thank God," his wife said. "I couldn't stand another Arizona summer."

When Francisco Vasquez de Coronado explored Arizona in 1540, he sent Spanish sea captain Hernando Alarcon up the Colorado with supplies, hoping they could link up. They missed each other by 300 miles, but Alarcon did take two longboats to the point where the Gila enters the Colorado, the site of today's Yuma.

The river crossing there played a critical role in the history of the West. The Spanish used it sporadically. But when they tried to secure the crossing, giving themselves a land route to California, they shot themselves in the foot.

Catholic missionaries established two missions in the Yuma area, and made friends with many of the natives. But then Spain sent soldiers to bolster the settlement, and the arrogant commander alienated the

Indians. Soldiers appropriated farms and crops, and let their horses eat the mesquite beans that the Indians relied on for flour. So in the summer of 1781 the Indians wiped out the Spaniards, including the missionaries.

Americans used the crossing to help conquer California during the Mexican War, and to reach the California gold fields in 1849 and 1850. Mexicans from Sonora also used the crossing to seek gold in California.

Several entrepreneurs ran ferries at Yuma, and robbers lurked nearby to waylay travelers. The U.S. Army established the outpost that would become Fort Yuma on the California shore. Sporadically, a town grew up where Yuma is today.

Steamboats began to navigate the river in 1852, carrying supplies for mines, towns and army camps in the interior of Arizona, as well as mines on both banks of the river. Ships from San Francisco unloaded freight in the estuary where the Colorado joins the Gulf of California, one hundred miles south of Yuma. From there, shallow-draft stern-wheelers and their barges took the provisions upriver. The steamboats plied the river until 1916, although their importance diminished from 1877 through 1881, when the Southern Pacific Railroad crossed Arizona. An army quartermaster depot and customs house were built on the Arizona side, where the town of Yuma was growing; they are now part of an Arizona state historic park.

In wet seasons the boats went far beyond the present site of Hoover Dam. Mormon Church President Brigham Young established a riverport at Callville, in case hostilities with the U.S. government should force him to bring supplies up from the Gulf of California. Callville was seat of Arizona's Pah-Ute County, which Congress took away in 1867 to form the southern tip of Nevada. Too bad.

In drier seasons, however, the Colorado was not nearly so navigable. Browne reported, "The little steamer which plies between the fort and the mouth of the river, distant one hundred miles, could not make the round trip up in less than two weeks, owing to the shoals and shifting bars. Up to La Paz and Fort Mojave the navigation was still worse. Twenty or thirty days up and down was considered a fair trip. The miners in that region were suffering for supplies, although six hundred tons of freight lay at the embarcadera awaiting transportation."

Martha Summerhayes, an army officer's bride who rode the steamboat Gila to Fort Mohave in 1874, wrote a detailed account of the hot, eighteen-day journey from Yuma to Mohave, including this account of the dinner menu: "The fare was meagre of course; fresh biscuit without butter, very salty boiled beef, and some canned vegetables, which were poor enough in those days. Pies made from preserved peaches or plums generally followed this delectable course…"

Both Browne and Summerhayes found Yuma an oasis of civilization in the wilderness. Both remarked on the welcome glasses of lemonade that greeted them there.

And Browne wrote, "The climate in winter is finer than that of Italy. It would scarcely be possible to suggest an improvement. I never experienced such exquisite Christmas weather as we enjoyed during our soujourn."

Not long ago, two elderly men from the upper Midwest were jawing at each other, as old friends will. One threatened to escape the other's company by spending the following winter in a more populous "snowbird" haven near Phoenix.

"No you won't," his friend laughed. "They'd run right over you in the traffic up there."

And so the old friends, and many thousand others, come to Yuma from Canada and the upper midwest to seek the winter sunshine and a little elbow room. The area is still the strongest citrus-growing area in Arizona; most of the orchards are on Yuma Mesa, above the river and the town.

The winter visitors' conversation took place during an excursion on the Yuma Valley Railroad, a tiny tourist line. Its lone switch engine and one or two coaches travel on abandoned Southern Pacific tracks that parallel the Colorado River south of Yuma, along the Lower Yuma Valley.

If Arizona is drawn as a human profile, as some cartoonists have done, the caricature's prominent chin is the fertile lower Yuma Valley, irrigated since 1916 by water from Laguna Dam, a few miles above Yuma.

The train stopped for coffee and pop at a Cocopah Indian village. Then it traveled on through the fields. One of the most striking sights was a huge field of Chinese cabbage, flowering and going to seed. The seeds will be in the hands of farmers in colder climates in time for spring planting. Yuma has long been a seed-growing center for a variety of vegetables.

Yuma is conscious of both its historic heritage and its Hispanic heritage, and has begun to go public with them both. Restored buildings along the riverfront are now a state park, and the Arizona Historical Society's Century House museum downtown celebrates all of Yuma's history. On the hill above the river, the notorious old Yuma Territorial Prison also is a popular state park.

At Yuma and up river at Parker, annual innertube float races go where the sternwheelers used to go. Laguna, the first dam on the river, and above it Imperial Dam, create recreation lakes and wildlife refuges. Inland, east of the river, stark, mysterious mountains rise against the sky.

The Kofa range, northeast of Yuma, was named by the acronym of the King of Arizona Mine, stenciled on boxes of supplies bound for that remote, vanished bonanza. (The name replaced an earlier, unprintable name based on the mountains' resemblance to an outhouse.) The mountain range now harbors rare desert bighorn sheep and specimens of the only palm trees native to Arizona.

Vegetation seems sparser in this part of Arizona, and the mountains both more forbidding and alluring. In territorial days this was the habitat of tough, individualistic burro prospectors and shoestring mining promoters. During World War II, U.S. tanks and ground soldiers maneuvered on these deserts, which were part of General George S. Patton's Desert Training Center. Now hundreds of thousands of winter visitors and rockhounds come to prowl the desert or rest in the sunshine. Residents and former residents of the village of Salome gather each September for a parade, dance and barbecue in honor of Dick Wick Hall,

who founded the town in 1904 and made it moderately famous.

Hall was a promoter, newspaperman, humorist and, until he founded Salome, a wanderer. He ran the Laughing Gas Station for early motorists, and started a sort of newspaper called the *Salome Sun*, "Made With A Laugh On A Mimeograph."

Hall populated Salome with fictional characters, including his pet frog who was seven years old and had never learned to swim. Hall contended the scorpion was simply a lobster, left over from ancient inland seas, who had lived in the desert too long. Hall also invented the hilarious Greasewood Lynx Golf Course, a 23-mile-long fictional course where cowboys caddied with pack mules.

The Saturday Evening Post began to print Hall's humor, and he was syndicated by many newspapers. But Hall had a semi-serious side, and he wrote: "Out here in the desert you don't need much—and you don't get much either—and after a while you get so as you don't want much—and when you get that way there ain't much use in going somewhere else. A man can put in a good deal of time setting and looking out across the desert, past miles and miles of greasewood and through the wriggly heat waves of the sunburned mountains in the distance, setting there just the same as you are, waiting for something to happen."

Many winter visitors, a lot of them farmers from Canada and the northern United States, come in winter to contemplate the desert. Nearby Quartzsite is better known for its winter explosion of residents in recreation vehicles, and its desert rat swap meets.

Interstate 10, carrying travelers from Phoenix to Los Angeles, runs past Quartzsite and crosses the river at Ehrenberg. This was a historic river port. Sternwheelers unloaded supplies and mining equipment here, and freight wagons, drawn by teams of twelve to twenty mules, delivered the goods inland to Prescott, Wickenburg, even Phoenix. Nearby and a bit upstream was La Paz, one of Arizona Territory's first mining boom towns—until the river shifted its course and the gold ran out.

Another bridge crosses the river at Parker, midway up Arizona's

Scenic Red Rock Crossing

profile. Joe and Nellie Bush still ran steam ferry boats here in 1934, when the Metropolitan Water District of Los Angeles built Parker Dam.

Arizona Governor Benjamin Mouer wanted the courts to decide how the water should be divided between the states before any more dams were built on the Colorado. He sent the Arizona National Guard to stop construction. Nellie Bush took the soldiers to the dam site, earning her the tongue-in-cheek title of commodore of the Arizona Navy. One of her boats became entangled in cables across the river, and the soldiers had to be rescued by construction workers working for "the enemy."

Parker Dam was completed, but the Interior Department and the courts began to deal with division of river water. After nearly thirty years of litigation, and nearly five years of congressional maneuvering, Arizona was authorized in 1968 to build the Central Arizona Project. Now the project carries water from behind Parker Dam to the central valleys of the state.

The Parker Strip, between Parker and the foot of the dam, is a busy recreation area for Arizonans and Californians who like to fish and waterski. They keep a number of second homes here—cabins and mobile homes, mostly.

The lake behind Parker Dam is called Lake Havasu, and an odd but delightful bit of the world has been created on its shores. Site Six was a World War II recreation area for Army Air Corps flying cadets at bases in western Arizona. In the 1960s the McCulloch Corporation, which makes chain saws and outboard motors, bought Site Six and began the planned community of Lake Havasu City.

McCulloch bought part of historic London Bridge, which was being replaced in England, and shipped it to the lake front. The bridge crosses a lagoon to a tiny Olde English village, one of the prime tourist attractions at Lake Havasu.

Interstate 40 crosses the river between Topock, Arizona and Needles, California. So does the Santa Fe Railroad. The crossing is flanked by the Havasu National Wildlife refuge, including Topock Gorge and Topock Swamp, and the Fort Mohave Indian Reservation. The original fort was a desert outpost. Today, farms of the Mohaves form a green band along both sides of the Colorado.

All of western Arizona is dotted with ghost towns. One of the liveliest, and most accessible, is Oatman at the foot of the Black Mountains. Gold mines flourished here early in this century, then petered out. Oatman is enjoying something of a revival, although it is still a very small town.

Burros roam the narrow main street, which was once part of U.S. 66. Visitors may think the burros were placed there for their benefit, but miners who worked the night shift at the Tom Reed Mine back in 1907 complained that the braying of the burros interrupted their daytime sleep.

Some of Oatman's buildings are trapezoidal, rather than square, tucked into the narrow space between main street and a canyon wall. Many of the buildings were made of corrugated tin, the material that tamed the West. In fact, even the interior walls upstairs in the Oatman Hotel and Museum are made of corrugated tin.

The town also has a rare example of an old U.S. 66 tourist court from the 1920s, when U.S. highways were first assigned numbers.

Back on the river bank, it's just a few miles up Arizona 95 to Bullhead City, a strip town with a main street fourteen miles long. Bullhead came into existence when Davis Dam was built after World War II, backing water up into El Dorado Canyon. The town is not named for its stubborn people, or the ground-hugging "sticker" that plagued me during my barefoot boyhood. It was named for a rock, shaped like the head of a bull, covered by the waters of the dam. Until recently, its greatest claim to fame was that it often reported the hottest temperature in the nation.

On the porch of a Mexican restaurant in mid-town Bullhead City, a small monument tells visitors that this was the site of Hardyville, a riverport of the 1860s and 1870s. William Hardy built the port to tranship goods from San Francisco, sending them on by wagon to the territorial capital at Prescott and the Army posts in the region.

Hardyville was the practical head of navigation on the Colorado. In wet seasons, boats could go far up the river, serving the mines in El

Dorado Canyon. And they went even farther, to tiny towns now vanished under Lake Mead, formed when Boulder (Hoover) Dam was completed in 1936. But most years, the freight stopped in Hardyville, since overrun by Bullhead City.

Bullhead is splitting at the seams now because of a phenomenon across the river: Laughlin, Nevada, and its gambling casinos. Rancher Don Laughlin started the place in the 1960s with one small bar and casino; the first patrons came across the river in small boats.

Now Laughlin has surpassed Lake Tahoe as a gaming center, and is closing fast on Reno. Tour buses full of gamblers even come to Laughlin from Las Vegas. The river has been bridged, but small boats carry gamblers between casinos, and across the river.

One of the big casinos is a monster replica of a river steamboat, maybe ten times the size of the boats that so laboriously navigated the Colorado. But you also can board a smaller, diesel-powered replica and cruise downriver sixty miles to Lake Havasu City, retracing the route of earlier explorers and gamblers who rode the river.

The Colorado River—one of Arizona's natural attributes—has served as the life blood and a relentless foe. With the ebb and flow of the tempermental Colorado, the earliest inhabitants learned to tame the beast.

And among the daring people who settled the distinctively western land called Arizona, the ranchers seem to have become symbolic of the place. They manipulated the Colorado, funneling its water to refresh their livestock and replenish the land. They proved that pioneers could survive, adapt, improvise, learn to feed themselves and prosper.

CANDIES & COOKIES

Downtown Tucson—contrasts between old and new

Oatmeal Cookies

½ cup margarine, softened

1 cup Crockett's Honey

1 egg

1 tsp vanilla

1½ cups Silver Creek Mill Stone Ground Whole Wheat Flour

½ tsp baking powder

½ tsp baking soda

½ tsp cinnamon

¼ tsp ground cloves

2 cups quick cooking oatmeal

½ cup raisins

½ cup Country Estate Pecan Meal

- Preheat oven to 350 degrees.
- Cream together margarine and honey.
- Beat in egg and vanilla; add flour, baking powder, baking soda, cinnamon and cloves; mix thoroughly.
- Fold in oatmeal.
- Add raisins and pecan meal.
- Bake 10-12 minutes on greased baking sheet.
- Makes 3 doz.

Cornstacks

4 cups Kachina Popcorn Caramel Corn

1 cup Wold's Peanuts

1 cup chow mein noodles

1 (12 oz) pkg chocolate chips

- Mix together caramel corn, peanuts and noodles in large bowl.
- Melt chocolate chips and pour over caramel corn mixture; toss until well mixed.
- Place spoonfuls of caramel corn mixture on waxed paper; cool.
- Store in covered container.
- Makes 7-8 cups.

White Chocolate-Corn Delight Cookies

1½ lbs white chocolate

2 cups Wold's Salted Peanuts

2 cups crushed Kachina Popcorn Caramel Corn

2 cups crushed Kachina Popcorn White Popcorn

- In saucepan, melt white chocolate.
- Mix in remaining ingredients.
- Drop by teaspoonfuls onto waxed paper; let cool at room temperature.
- Makes 6 cups.

Pecan-Topped Toffee

1 cup butter

1 cup firmly packed brown sugar

6 (1.375 oz) bars milk chocolate

½ cup finely chopped Country Estate Pecans

- In deep, narrow saucepan, combine butter and sugar.
- Cook over medium high heat, stirring constantly, until mixture reaches exactly 300 degrees on candy thermometer (hard crack stage).
- Pour immediately into greased 9″ square baking pan.
- Lay chocolate bars evenly over hot candy. When soft, spread into smooth layer.
- Sprinkle nuts over chocolate; press in lightly with fingers.
- Chill in refrigerator 1 hour.
- Invert candy onto flat surface; break apart into small, irregular pieces.
- Makes 12-15 pieces.

Cactus Candy

2 envs plain gelatin	• Soften gelatin in water.
½ cup water	• Heat syrup and salt until boiling.
1 cup Cheri's Prickly Pear Syrup	• Add gelatin to hot syrup; stir until dissolved.
⅛ tsp salt	
powdered sugar	• Boil slowly 5 minutes.
	• Pour into 8″ square pan. Allow to set 10 hours.
	• Cut candy into small squares; roll in powdered sugar.
	• Makes 64 squares.

Basic Pecan Pralines

4 cups sugar, divided	• Mix 3 cups sugar, salt and cream together.
1 tsp salt	
2 cups cream	• Melt remaining cup sugar very slowly in heavy skillet, stirring constantly, until caramel-colored and syrupy.
3 cups The Pecan Store Pecan Halves	
	• Pour sugar and cream mixture into syrup all at once; stir vigorously.
	• Boil, without stirring, until syrup reaches soft ball stage, 234 degrees on candy thermometer.
	• Add pecans; stir quickly for several seconds.
	• Drop by spoonfuls onto waxed paper to form flat, round patties.
	• Makes 1½ doz.

No Bake Date Balls

1 cup chunky peanut butter
1 cup chopped Sphinx Medjool Dates
1 cup powdered sugar
½ lb white chocolate bark

- Mix well first 3 ingredients; form into balls.
- Melt white chocolate bark in double boiler.
- Dip balls; place on foil.
- Refrigerate until firm.
- Makes 40 balls.

Mud Balls

¼ cup peanut butter
¼ cup Malcolm's Honey
¼ cup wheat germ
½ cup oatmeal
¼ cup chocolate chips
½ cup coconut
½ cup chopped Sphinx Dates

- Combine peanut butter and honey.
- Heat until melted.
- Add remaining ingredients.
- Roll into balls; refrigerate 3-6 hours.
- Makes 32 balls.

Dingbats

1½ cups chopped Sphinx Dates
1 cup sugar
¼ cup Carnation® Butter
1 egg, beaten
⅛ tsp salt
1 tsp vanilla
3 cups crispy rice cereal
1 cup chopped nuts
coconut

- Cook dates, sugar and butter in heavy saucepan 5 minutes.
- Remove from heat; add remaining ingredients.
- When cool, roll into balls; roll balls in coconut, chill.
- Makes 3 doz.

Thumbprint Jalapeno Cookies

⅔ cup margarine
½ cup firmly packed brown sugar
1 egg, separated
½ tsp vanilla
1½ cups all-purpose flour
1 cup finely chopped The Pecan Store Pecans
¾ cup Desert Kettle Jalapeno Jelly

- Cream margarine, sugar, egg yolk and vanilla.
- Add flour, mix until dough holds together.
- Shape into walnut size balls.
- Dip balls into slightly beaten egg white; drain briefly, roll in nuts.
- Place 1″ apart on ungreased baking sheet.
- With thumb, press a well in center of each ball.
- Bake at 350 degrees 10 minutes; remove. Press thumbprint back and fill with jelly.
- Bake until jelly melts, 5-10 minutes.
- Makes 3 doz.

Cherry Nut Brownies

1 (8 oz) ctn Carnation® Smooth 'n' Creamy Cherry Yogurt, divided
1 (21.5 oz) pkg brownie mix
1 egg
½ cup chopped walnuts
⅓ cup chopped maraschino cherries
¾ cup semi-sweet chocolate pieces
3 tbsp Carnation® Butter
1½ cups sifted powdered sugar

- Stir yogurt in carton.
- Combine brownie mix, ½ cup yogurt and egg. Mix according to pkg directions.
- Stir in walnuts and cherries.
- Spread in 9″ x 13″ x 2″ well buttered baking pan.
- Bake in 350 degree oven 25-30 minutes; cool.
- Melt chocolate pieces and butter; cool thoroughly.
- Blend in remaining yogurt and the powdered sugar. Beat well to spreading consistency.
- Spread on brownies.
- Makes 16-20 brownies.

Jelly Tots

½ cup white or brown sugar

½ cup butter, softened

1 tsp vanilla

2 Hickman's Eggs

2½ cups sifted all-purpose flour

2 tsp baking powder

½ tsp salt

1 egg white, slightly beaten

1 cup Country Estate Pecan Meal

Cheri's Arizona Red Lime Marmalade, Pomegranate Jelly, Prickly Pear Jelly or Tucson Sunny Citrus Marmalade

- Preheat oven to 375 degrees.
- Cream together sugar and butter.
- Beat in vanilla, eggs, flour, baking powder and salt.
- Roll dough into ball.
- Chill briefly. Pinch off pieces; roll into 1" balls.
- Roll balls in egg white then pecan meal.
- Place on lightly greased and floured baking sheet; bake 5 minutes.
- Depress center of each cookie with thumb.
- Continue baking until done, about 8 minutes.
- When cool, fill indentations with jelly or marmalade.
- Makes 3½ doz.

BUYER'S GUIDE

Bakery (Breads, Cookies, Crackers)

Arizona Baking Company, Tucson
Arizona French Bakery, Tempe
Bagel Baker, Inc., Phoenix
Best Buy Foods, Inc., Phoenix
Blair Bakery Products, Prescott
Cafe Valley, Phoenix
Cake Arts Mfg. Company, Phoenix
Cowboy Vittles & More (Cowboy), Scottsdale
El Zarape Mexican Foods, Inc., Tucson
Estrella Tortilla Factory, Inc., Phoenix
Foster's, J. L., Tucson
French Loaf, Tucson
Great Harvest, Phoenix
Holsum Bakery, Inc. (Holsum), Phoenix
Italian Bakery, Inc., Phoenix
Karsh's Bakery, Phoenix
Knolan's Bakery, Phoenix
La Joyeux, Inc., Tucson
LeCave's Bakery, Inc., Tucson
Lujans Pasteries, Tucson
Mannons Chocolates, Inc. (Old Pueblo, Mannons), Tubac
Meyers Bakery, Arizona City
Middle Eastern Bakery & Deli, Inc., Phoenix
Milestone Bakery, Mayer
Napoli Italian Bakery, Chandler
Penny's Parlor, Tempe
Rainbo Baking Company of Phoenix (Rainbo), Phoenix
Rainbo Baking Company (Rainbo), Tucson
Red Eagle Enterprises, Inc. (Red Eagle), Surprise
Sclortino's Italian Bakery, Tucson
SHEA-NA Foods, Phoenix
Small Planet Bakery (Small Planet), Tucson
Snyder's Dutch Soft Pretzels, Phoenix
Steele Homestyle Baking Company, C. (C. Steele Homestyle), Phoenix
Upper Crust, Phoenix
Valley Pie Company, Inc., Phoenix
Van De Kamp's Holland Dutch Bakers, Inc., Los Angeles, CA

Beverages

Casa Grande Enterprises, Inc. (Pepsi Cola), Casa Grande
Coca-Cola Bottling Company, Douglas
Coca-Cola Bottling Company of Northern Arizona, Flagstaff
Commers Conditioned Water, Tempe
Cowboy Vittles & More (Cowboy), Scottsdale
Crystal Bottled Waters, Phoenix
Espressions Coffees and Teas (Espressions), Tempe
Jackson's Foremost Foods (Jackson, Foremost), Phoenix
Kalil Bottling Company (Royal Crown, Dr Pepper, Squirt, Hires, Canada Dry, Big Red, Crest, Lipton Tea), Tucson
Name Brands, Inc., Prescott
National Coffee Service, Scottsdale
Natural Enterprises, Tucson
Natural Life Foods (Fresh Pic Juices), Phoenix
Pepsi Cola Bottling Company, Flagstaff
Pepsi Cola Bottling Company, Phoenix
Phoenix Distributing Co., Inc., Phoenix
Quality Fresh Juice, Tucson
Santa Rita Bottling Company, Tucson
Seven-Up Bottling Company of Tucson, Tucson
Seven-Up/Like Cola Bottling Company, Phoenix
Shasta, Phoenix
Sun Orchard, Tempe
Sun Valley Beverage, Inc., Yuma
Sunburst Foods, Phoenix
Sunset Food and Beverage, Phoenix

Candy

Bevell, Payson
Cactus Candy Company, Phoenix
Cahill Desert Products Company (Cahill Desert Products), Phoenix
Cake Arts Mfg. Company, Phoenix
Camelot Mfg., Lake Havasue City
Cerreta Candy Co., Phoenix
Champion Chip, Inc., Tucson
Choc-Alot, Tucson
Chocolate Creations, Mesa
Concession Foods Company, Phoenix
Copper Country Fudge, Jerome
Coyote Kates, Carefree
Designer Lollipops, Mesa
Gollipops, Inc., Payson
International Fine Candies, Phoenix
Licker Company, The, Winslow
Mannons (Old Pueblo, Mannons), Tubac
Morley Candy Makers West, Tempe
Sugar Shack, Tucson
Sunset Food and Beverage Corp, Phoenix
Tuckett Candy Company, Inc., Mesa
Truffles by James, Tucson
Ventures West, Tempe
Wold's Snack Foods (Wold's), Chandler

Canned Foods

Arizona Products, Inc., Yuma
Beatrice Hunt Wesson, Inc., Fullerton
Fiesta Canning Co., Inc., Phoenix
Rosarita Mexican Foods (Rosarita), Mesa

Eggs/Cheese/Dairy Products

Acson Corporation, Scottsdale
Arizona Egg Company (Laid in Arizona), Casa Grande
Carnation Dairy (Carnation), Phoenix
Cowboy Vittles & More (Cowboy), Scottsdale
Crowther Distributing, Springerville
Heartland Dairy Restaurant, Tempe
Hickman Egg Ranch (Hickman's), Glendale
Hidden Villa, Phoenix
Imports, Ltd., Scottsdale
InstantWhip-Arizona, Inc. (instantwhip), Phoenix
Jackson's Foremost Foods (Jackson, Foremost), Phoenix
La Corona Foods, Glendale
Olson Farms, Tucson
Resser's Fine Foods, Inc., Beaverton
Safeway Stores, Inc., Tempe
Shamrock Foods (Shamrock), Phoenix
Shamrock Foods (Shamrock), Tucson
Ultra Products Corporation, Tempe
United Dairymen of Arizona, The (UDA Seal of Arizona), Tempe

Ethnic

East Meats West Italia, Tempe
El Molino Tamales, Phoenix
Food Products Corporation (Arizona Brand), Phoenix
Grande Tortilla Factory, Tucson
La Canasta Mexican Food, Inc., Phoenix
La Suprema Mexican Foods, Tucson
Mi Casa Tortilla Factory, Safford
Middle Eastern Bakery Deli, Phoenix
Mission-ARGA's Mexican Food Products, Tempe
Napoli Italian Bakery, Chandler
R & S Mexican Foods, Glendale
Rainbo Baking Company, Phoenix
Rosarita Mexican Foods (Rosarita), Mesa
Tamale Factory, The, Glendale
Tamales Land, The, Tucson
Territorial Gourmet Foods, Inc. (Territorial Gourmet), Tucson

Ethnic Bakery

Alejandro's Tortilla, Tucson
Bel France, Scottsdale
El Zarape Mexican Foods, Tucson
El Porvinar Tortilla Factory, Superior
Estrella Tortilla Factory, Inc., Phoenix
Food Products Corp. (Arizona Brand), Phoenix
La Canasta Mexican Food Products, Phoenix
La Palmita, Inc., Avandale
La Patisserie, Phoenix
La Paloma Tortilleria, Tucson
La Tolteca, Phoenix
Lucy's Tortilla Factory, Mesa
Luly's Tortilleria, Nogales
Mi Casita Tortilla, Tucson
Mission-ARGA's Mexican Food, Tempe
Mi Ranchito, Phoenix
Ochoa's Tortilla Factory, Casa Grande
Red Eagle Enterprises, Surprise
Sahuarita Tortilla Factory, Sahuarita
Solamente, Inc., Tucson
Tortilla Factory of Tucson, Tucson
Villas Tortillas, Sierra Vista
Yaqui Tortilla Factory, Tucson

Fish/Seafoods, Canned and Cured

European Meat Products, Inc., Phoenix
Paradise Food Brokerage, Inc., Phoenix
Schifano Food Sales, Inc., Tucson

Fish/Seafoods, Fresh and Frozen

Arizona Fish Company, Payson
G & G Food Sales, Inc., Phoenix
Romo, R. L., Inc., Nogales
Schifano Food Sales, Inc., Tucson
United Fisheries, Safford

Flour/Corn Meal/Mixes

Baystate Milling Company, Tempe
Best Buy Foods, Inc., Phoenix
La Canasta Mexican Food, Inc., Phoenix
Maria's Corporation, Tempe
Mannons (Old Pueblo, Mannons), Tubac
Monika's Bakery (The Honey Baker), Tucson
Silver Creek Mill (Silver Creek Mill), Snowflake
Territorial Gourmet Foods, Inc. (Territorial Gourmet), Tucson

Food Preparations

Arizona Brand Nutritionals, Inc., Tempe
Arizona Products, Inc., Yuma
Clover Club Foods Company, Phoenix
Country Fare Caterers, Inc., Phoenix
Crispy's Inc., Tucson
The Dial Corporation, Phoenix
El Molino Tamales, Phoenix
El Zarape Mexican Foods, Inc., Tucson
Food Products Corp. (Arizona Brand), Phoenix
Frito Lay, Inc., Casa Grande
Gomez Tortilla Factory, Miami
Grande Tortilla Factory, Inc., Tucson
H & PC Products, Inc., Phoenix
International Fine Foods, Scottsdale
La Bonita Food Products, Tucson
La Supreme Mexican Foods, Inc., Tucson
La Tolteca Mexican Foods, Inc., Phoenix
La Reyna Tortilla Factory, Tucson
Mi Casa Tortilla Factory, Safford
Mission-ARGA's Mexican Food Products, Tempe
Ochoa's Tortilla Factory, Casa Grande
Pink Saguaro Gourmet Foods, Tucson
R & S Mexican Food Products, Inc., Glendale
SHEA-NA Foods, Phoenix
Saguaro Potato Chip Company, Inc., Tucson

Santa Cruz Chili & Spice Company (Santa Cruz), Tumacacori
Southwest Design & Supply Company, Phoenix
Sunland Foods, Tucson
Tamales Land, The, Tucson

Frozen Foods/Desserts

Arizona Products, Inc., Yuma
Baskin-Robbins, Inc. (Baskin-Robbins), Glendale
Carnation Dairies (Carnation), Phoenix
Cathy's Rum Cake Caterers
Coyle Ice Cream, Inc., Mary, Phoenix
Frigid Products Company, Phoenix
Instantwhip-Arizona, Inc. (instantwhip), Phoenix
McClain, Tom, Company, Inc., The, Phoenix
Penguins Place Frozen Yogurt (Penguins), Buena Park
Shamrock Foods Company (Shamrock), Tucson
Shamrock Foods Company (Shamrock), Phoenix
Sunland Foods (Sunland Foods), Tucson
Territorial Gourmet Foods, Inc. (Territorial Gourmet), Tucson

Gift Baskets

Cheri's Desert Harvest (Cheri's), Tucson
Cowboy Vittles & More (Cowboy), Scottsdale
Desert Kettle (Desert Kettle), Fountain Hills
Mannons (Old Pueblo, Mannons), Tubac
Marvelous Morsels, Scottsdale

Honey/Syrup/Sugar

Arizona Cattle Industries, Inc., Phoenix
Cahill Desert Products Company (Cahill Desert Products), Phoenix
Cheri's Desert Harvest (Cheri's), Tucson
Cowboy Vittles & More (Cowboy), Scottsdale
Crockett-Stewart Honey Company, Inc. (Crockett's), Tempe
Flagstaff Honey (Flagstaff), Flagstaff
Green Valley Arizona Pecans (Chaparral), Sahuarita
Malcolm's Honey Company (Malcolm's), Tucson
Mountain Top Honey Co. (Mountain Top), Flagstaff

Jams/Jellies

Arnold Pickle & Olive Company (Arnold's), Phoenix
Cactus Candy Company, Phoenix
Cahill Desert Products Company (Cahill Desert Products), Phoenix
Cheri's Desert Harvest (Cheri's), Tucson
Country Rose, Tucson
Cowboy Vittles & More (Cowboy), Scottsdale
Crowther Distributing, Springerville
Desert Kettle (Desert Kettle), Fountain Hills
Natural Life Foods (Natural), Phoenix
New England Apple Products Company, Inc., Littleton
Rocking R, Tucson
Sallie's Seasonings (Sallie's), Phoenix
Sugar's Kitchen (Arizona Champagne Sauces), Tucson
Sunset Food and Beverage Corp., Phoenix
Valbur, Inc., Tucson

Meats/Meat Products

Arizona Beef Co., Phoenix
Bar-S Foods Company (Bar-S), Phoenix
Barone Sausages (Barone Sausages), Tucson
Beck's Sulphur Springs Meat Packers, Inc. (Beck's), Cochise
Beefway Ranch, Chino Valley
Bob's Butcher Shop, Flagstaff
Briden Foods, Inc., Glendale
Busby Meat Company, Tucson
Canyon Provisions, Inc., Tempe
Carpenters Meat Packing, Valley Farms
Chicken House, Somerton
Country Beef, Winkleman
Crocketts, Inc., Phoenix
Evan Meat Company, Phoenix

Farmer John Meats, Phoenix
Firpo Poultry, H., Phoenix
Henry's Corned Beef, Inc., Phoenix
George's Meat Processing, Elfrida
Gillum Meat Co., Buckeye
Goldmark Foods, Inc. (Goldmark), Phoenix
Gourmet Foods European Meat Products, Inc., Phoenix
Hormel Meats, Phoneix
Lory Meat Company, Inc., Glendale
Malapai Meat Packing, Taylor
Maricopa Packing, Phoenix
Max's Food Processing, Phoenix
Pinal Meat Packing, Maricopa
Post Meats, Dan, Tucson
Reeser's Fine Foods, Inc., Beaverton
Rocking R, Tuscon
San Pedro Custom Meats, St. David
Schreiners Fine Sausage (Schreiner's), Phoenix
Sherwood and Hales, Springerville
Snowflake Packing Co., Snowflake
Southwest Meat & Provisions, Phoenix
Spurlock Meat Investment Livestock Enterprises, Mesa
Stone's Meat Packing, Mesa
Sulphur Springs Meat Packer, Cochise
Suncrest Poultry Farms, Phoenix
Sunland Beef, Tollesoh
Thomas Locker, Chandler
Tucson Meat, Tucson
Tyson Gourmet Meats, Phoenix
Valbur, Inc., Tucson
Valley Meat Co., Yuma
Valley Meat Packing, Safford
Valley Wholesale Meat Co., Peoria
VelMar Food Services, Inc., Phoenix
Western Meat Company, Laveen
Westhar, Inc., Tucson
White Tank Meat Processors, Litchfield Park
Willcox Packing House, Willcox
Young's Farm (Young's Farm), Dewey

Miscellaneous

Cinnabar Specialty Foods., Inc. (Cinnabar), Prescott
Instantwhip-Arizona, Inc. (instantwhip), Phoenix
Ocotillo Southwest Flavors, Tucson
Pink Saguaro Gourmet Foods, Tucson
Zefco Foods, Tucson

Nuts/Seeds

Arizona Nuts (Arizona Nuts), Tucson
Arizona Pistachio Company, The (The Arizona Pistachio Company), Tucson
Cheri's Desert Harvest (Cheri's), Tucson
Country Estate Pecans (Country Estate), Sahuarita
Farmer's Investment Co., Sahuarita
Green Valley Arizona Pecans (The Pecan Store), Sahuarita
Small Planet Bakery (Small Planet), Tucson
Triple A Pistachio (Triple A Pistachio), Cochise
Wold's Snack Foods (Wold's), Chandler

Pasta/Noodles

The Creamette Company (Creamette, Creamettes), Tolleson
De Cio Pasta (De Cio Pasta), Cave Creek
European Meat Products, Inc., Phoenix
Italian Bakery, Inc., Phoenix
International Fine Foods, Scottsdale
Ladson Noodle Company (Ladson's), Tucson
Michael's Ravioli & Pasta, Tucson
Sciortino's Italian, Tucson
Territorial Gourmet Foods, Inc. (Territorial Gourmet), Tucson

Poultry

Arizona Egg Company, Casa Grande
Firpo Poultry, H., Phoenix

Pilgrims Pride, Phoenix
Suncrest Poultry Farms, Inc., Phoenix
Young's Farm (Young's Farm), Dewey

Produce/Canned, Frozen and Preserved

Anaheim Citrus Products Company, Yuma
Arnold Pickle & Olive Company (Arnold's), Phoenix
Cactus Candy Company, Phoenix
Cahill Desert Products Company (Cahill Desert Products), Phoenix
Cheri's Desert Harvest (Cheri's), Tucson
Cinnabar Specialty Foods, Inc. (Cinnabar), Prescott
Crowther Distributing, Springerville
Fiesta Canning Company, Inc., McNeal
Francies Date Company, Phoenix
Imports, Ltd., Scottsdale
Milani Foods, Melrose Park
New England Apple Products Company, Inc., Littleton
Pima Western, Inc., Tucson
Resser's Fine Foods, Inc., Beaverton
Sallie's Seasonings (Sallie's), Phoenix
Sunset Food and Beverage Corp., Phoenix
Valbur, Inc., Tucson

Produce, Fresh

Action Produce, Glendale
Anaheim Citrus, Yuma
Arizona Sun Products, Scottsdale
Attela Produce, Inc., Phoenix
Barelli Produce Distributors, Nogales
Bonita Valley Apple Co., Willcox
Bradley Produce, Phoenix
Browns Orchards (Brown's), Willcox
CAB Produce (Pavo), Nogales
Cherry's Arizona Harvest, Tucson
Ehrlichs Date Garden (Ehrlichs), Yuma
Everkrisp Vegetables, Phoenix
Francies Date Company, Phoenix
Fresh Citrus, Tempe
J & J Citrus, Phoenix
J. R. Norton, Phoenix
King's Onion House, Phoenix
Mesa Citrus, Mesa
Munson Date Co (Munson's), Tucson
Navajo Marketing, Glendale
Rascon Vegetables, Wilcox
Sphinx Date Ranch (Sphinx), Phoenix
Sunkist (Sunkist), Sherman Oaks, CA
Sherill Farms, Roll
Tumbleweed Citrus, Mesa
Valley Farms Ltd. (Valley's Finest Apples), Willcox
Verde Growers, Yuma
J. A. Wood Co. (Copperhead), Phoenix
Young's Farm (Young's Farm), Dewey
Yuma Citrus Co., Yuma
Yuma Mesa Fruitgrowers, Yuma
Ziedl Produce, Phoenix

Sauces/Relishes/Dips

Arizona Pepper Products Co. (Arizona Gunslinger), Mesa
Arnold Pickle & Olive Co. (Arnold's), Phoenix
Cinnabar Specialty Foods, Inc. (Cinnabar), Prescott
Desert Rose Salsa (Desert Rose), Tucson
Fresh Citras Products, Tempe
J and S Foods (Big Juans), Phoenix
Jim's Spice Wholesale Mix Products, Phoenix
Bill Johnson BBQ (Big Apple), Glendale
Klein Kosher Pickle, Phoenix
Macayo's of Arizona, Phoenix
Mannons (Old Pueblo, Mannons), Tubac
Maria's Corporation, Tempe
Max's Food Processing, Phoenix
Miguel's Food Products (Miguel's), Tucson
Poblano Hot Sauce Company, Tucson
Rocking R, Tucson
Rosarita Mexican Foods (Rosarita), Mesa

Sallie's Seasonings (Sallie's), Phoenix
Santa Cruz Chili & Spice Company (Santa Cruz),
 Tumacacori
Sahuaro Spice Co. (Sahuaro Spice Co.), Phoenix
Southwestern Originals, Tucson
Sugar's Kitchen (Arizona Champagne), Tucson
Sunset Food and Beverage Corp., Phoenix
Territorial Gourmet Foods, Inc. (Territorial Gourmet),
 Tucson

Seasonings/Herbs/Chili Mixes

Fresh Touch Gardens (Fresh Touch Gardens), Peoria
Mad Coyote Spice Co. (Mad Coyote), Carefree
Mannons (Old Pueblo, Mannons), Tubac
Ocotillo Southwest Flavors, Tucson
Rhee's (Rhee's), Phoenix
Sallie's Seasonings (Sallie's), Phoenix
Santa Cruz Chili & Spice (Santa Cruz), Tumacacori
Sahuaro Spice Co. (Sahuaro Spice Co.), Phoenix
Sugar's Kitchen (Arizona Champagne Sauces, Arizona
 Southwest Mix), Tucson

Snack Foods

Best Buy Foods (Best Buy Foods), Phoenix
Champion Chip, Inc., Tucson
Chandler Eagle Foods, Chandler
Clover Club Foods (Clover Club), Phoenix
Crispy's, Inc. (Crispy's), Tucson
Didier & Sons, Yuma
Dueling Date Gardens, Yuma
Food Products Corp (Arizona Brand), Phoenix
Frito Lay, Inc., Casa Grande
Kachina Popcorn (Kachina Popcorn), Scottsdale
La Bonita Food Products, Tucson
Mi Ranchita, Phoenix
Netco, Maricopa
Poore Brothers, Inc. (Poore Brothers), Goodyear
Rosarita Mexican Foods (Rosarita), Mesa
Sage and Sand, Phoenix
Saguaro Potato Chip Co. (Saguaro), Tucson
Scudders, Laura (Laura Scudders), Phoenix
Territorial Gourmet Foods, Inc. (Territorial Gourmet),
 Tucson
Wold's Snack Foods (Wold's), Chandler

Soup Mixes

Anaheim Citrus Product Company, Yuma
Francies Date Company, Phoenix
Milani Foods, Melrose Park
Pima Western, Inc., Tucson
Territorial Gourmet Foods, Inc. (Territorial Gourmet),
 Tucson

Vegetable and Cooking Oil

Casa Grande Oil Mill, Casa Grande
Desert Whale Jojoba Company, Inc., Tucson
Janca's Jojoba Oil and Seed Company, Mesa
Western Cotton Services Corp., Phoenix

Wines/Beers

Arizona Vineyards (Arizona Vineyards), Nogales
Black Mountain Breweries, Cave Creek
Christopher Joseph Brewing Company, Inc. (Bandersnatch
 Milk Stout, Cardinal, Big Horn, Christopher Joseph),
 Tempe
Sonoita Vineyards, Elgin
Sun Valley Beverage, Inc., Yuma
Webb Winery, R. W., Inc. (R. W. Webb), Vail

INDEX

Crops Grown in Arizona

CROP	YIELD/ACRE	MONTHS OF AVAILABILITY

t, Melons and Nuts

›ples, Red Delicious	20 tons	September/October
›ples, Golden Delicious	20 tons	August/September
›ples, Granny-Smiths	30 tons	September/October
›ricots		May/June
›ntaloupe	450 ctns	September/October
	450 ctns	May/June
›apes	8 tons	May/July
›apefruit	16 tons	December/June
›neydew	557 ctns	September/October
	557 ctns	February
›mons	18 tons	October/February
›elons	850 ctns	September/October
›iscellaneous		September/October
›ctarines		May
›anges	12 tons	December/May
›aches		May
›ars		November/January
›cans	1 ton	November/January
›tachios	1 ton	September
›ums		May/June
›mpkins	12 tons	October
›ngerines	12 tons	November/April
›atermelon	20 tons	May/September

›ns

›arley	100 bu	May/July
›rn	113 bu	October/November
›rghum	87 bu	May/July
›heat, Durum	86 bu	May/July
›heat, Other	93 bu	May/July

›bs and Spices

›nise	350 ctns	January/March
›rgugula	470 ctns	November/April
›asil	800 ctns	May/November
›ay Leaf		June/July
›urnet		June/July
›hicory	520 ctns	December/March
›hives		December/March
›ilantro	570 ctns	December/March
›umin		December/March
›ill	600 ctns	December/March

Crops Grown in Arizona *(Continued)*

CROP	YIELD/ACRE	MONTHS OF AVAILABILITY

bs and Spices *(Continued)*

arlic	7 tons	June/July
eranium Scented		All Year
orehound		June/July
ysop		June/July
avender		All Year
emon Grass	800 ctns	May/November
emon Verbena		All Year
corice		June/July
arjoram	450 ctns	June/November
lint	700 ctns	May/October
regano	400 ctns	June/November
arsley	640 ctns	October/May
apini	240 ctns	December/April
osemary	600 ctns	March/December
ue		June/July
age		All Year
avory, Summer		June/July
avory, Winter		All Year
hallots		March/December
orrel, French		June/July
arragon (French)		June/November
hyme	500 ctns	March/December

getables

rtichoke	305 ctns	December/March
sparagus	100 ctns	October/February
eans, Green	5 ctns	May/June
eans, Fava	980 ctns	January/March
eans, Pinto	1700 lbs	November
eans, Teperary	1500 lbs	June
eets	265 ctns	November/April
ok Choy	625 ctns	November/January
roccoli	490 ctns	November/March
abbage, Green	365 ctns	November/May
auliflower	465 ctns	November/March
elery	224 ctns	January/March
arrots	235 ctns	December/July
hard, Swiss	375 ctns	November/March
orn, Mexican, June	1000 dzn	June
orn, Sweet	155 ctns	May/June
	155 ctns	October/November
ucumbers, Slicer	350 ctns	May/June
	350 ctns	October/November

Crops Grown in Arizona *(Continued)*

CROP	YIELD/ACRE	MONTHS OF AVAILABILITY

etables *(Continued)*

ucumbers, Pickle	5 tons	September/October
	5 tons	May/June
ggplant	550 ctns	June/July
ndive	250 ctns	October/April
scarole	245 ctns	October/April
reens, Kale	325 ctns	October/May
reens, Mustard	550 ctns	October/May
reens, Collard	470 ctns	October/May
reens, Turnip	475 ctns	October/May
reens, Japanese	400 ctns	October/April
ettuce, Bibb	770 ctns	November/April
ettuce, Boston	340 ctns	October/April
ettuce, Iceberg	770 ctns	October/December
ettuce, Leaf	475 ctns	October/April
ettuce, Romaine	590 ctns	October/April
eeks	750 ctns	January/April
apa	640 ctns	November/January
kra	270 ctns	June/October
nions, Dry	750 bags	May/June
nions, Green	955 ctns	November/July
nions, Transplants	1800 ctns	April
eas, Blackeye	2.2 tons	October/November
eppers, Chili	9.5 tons	June/October
eppers, Bell	555 ctns	May/November
opcorn	2 tons	August/September
otatoes, Sweet	12 tons	September/October
adishes	500 ctns	October/April
adishes, Japanese	600 ctns	December/March
oot, Celery	400 ctns	October/February
utabaga	410 ctns	December/April
pinach	300 ctns	October/April
quash, Summer	200 ctns	May/October
quash, Winter	450 ctns	July
omatoes	390 bu	October/June
urnips	450 ctns	June
egetables, Oriental	430 ctns	October/June

DISCOVERED TREASURES

A Reflection of ARIZONA COOKING

- A $19.95 value offered at a special discount of $16.95
- Arizona manufacturers coupons inside the book are valued over $20

Please send ___ copy (copies) of **DISCOVERED TREASURES A Reflection of ARIZONA COOKING** @ $16.95/copy, plus $2.50 freight to: (Make check or money order out to Leisure Time Publishing, 9029 Directors Row, Dallas, TX. 75247)

Name: _____

Address: _____

City/State/Zip:_____ Phone:_____

DISCOVERED TREASURES

A Reflection of ARIZONA COOKING

- A $19.95 value offered at a special discount of $16.95
- Arizona manufacturers coupons inside the book are valued over $20

Please send ___ copy (copies) of **DISCOVERED TREASURES A Reflection of ARIZONA COOKING** @ $16.95/copy, plus $2.50 freight to: (Make check or money order out to Leisure Time Publishing, 9029 Directors Row, Dallas, TX. 75247)

Name: _____

Address: _____

City/State/Zip:_____ Phone:_____

DISCOVERED TREASURES

A Reflection of ARIZONA COOKING

- A $19.95 value offered at a special discount of $16.95
- Arizona manufacturers coupons inside the book are valued over $20

Please send ___ copy (copies) of **DISCOVERED TREASURES A Reflection of ARIZONA COOKING** @ $16.95/copy, plus $2.50 freight to: (Make check or money order out to Leisure Time Publishing, 9029 Directors Row, Dallas, TX. 75247)

Name: _____

Address: _____

City/State/Zip:_____ Phone:_____